D.H. LAWRENCE

D. H. LAWRENCE

Neil Champion

Life and Works

Jane Austen
The Brontës
Thomas Hardy
Hemingway
D.H. Lawrence
Katherine Mansfield
George Orwell
Shakespeare
H.G. Wells
Virginia Woolf

Cover illustration by David Armitage

Series adviser: Dr Cornelia Cook
Series designer: David Armitage
Series editor: Susannah Foreman

First published in 1989 by
Wayland (Publishers) Ltd
61 Western Road, Hove
East Sussex BN3 1JD, England

British Library Cataloguing in Publication Data

Champion, Neil
  D. H. Lawrence.
  1. Fiction in English. Lawrence, D.H. (David Herbert),
  1885–1930 – Critical studies.
  I. Title   II. Series
  823'.912

ISBN 1–85210–422–8

Typeset by Kalligraphics Ltd, Horley, Surrey
Printed in Italy by G. Canale & C.S.p.A., Turin
Bound in the UK by MacLehose, Portsmouth

Contents

1 The Life of D.H. Lawrence

D. H. Lawrence was born in Victoria Street ('Hell Row'), Eastwood, in 1885. A plaque can be seen above the door of the mining cottage commemorating this event.

David Herbert Lawrence was born on 11 September 1885, into a mining family who lived in the village of Eastwood, situated about eight miles from the county town of Nottingham. He has left a vivid account of the area and what it meant to him to grow up amongst the mining families on the borders of great stretches of agricultural land.

A portrait of Lawrence as a man, painted in 1920 by Jan Juta. By this time, Lawrence had moved intellectually and spiritually away from his Midlands mining roots, but remained emotionally attached to the area all his life.

I was born . . . in Eastwood, a mining village of some thousand souls . . . one mile from the small stream, the Erewash, which divides Nottinghamshire from Derbyshire. It is hilly country, looking west to Crich and towards Matlock, sixteen miles away, and east and north-east towards Mansfield and the Sherwood Forest district. To me it seemed, and still does seem, an extremely beautiful countryside . . . To me, as a child and a young man, it was still the old England of the forest and agricultural past; there were no motor cars, the mines were, in a sense, an accident in the landscape, and Robin Hood and his merry men were not very far away.

(D. H. Lawrence, *Letters*, 1924)

His mother, Lydia Beardsall (who was to play such an important part in his development as both a man and a writer), had been a schoolteacher in Kent before her marriage to Arthur Lawrence. His father worked at the colliery in Brinsly and lived the hard, physically tiring and dangerous life of a coalminer. His parents'

7

Lawrence as a child (centre) photographed with his family. His mother (Lydia) and father (Arthur) are seated in the front row with Lettice Ada. In the back row are (left to right) Emily, George and William.

marriage was far from ideal, Lydia feeling socially and intellectually superior to the life of the mining community going on around her; her husband content with the companionship of the men he worked with, drinking, often excessively, with them on the way home from the pits.

Mother would wait up for him at night, her rage seething, until on his arrival it boiled over in a torrent of biting truths which turned him from his slightly fuddled and pleasantly apologetic mood into a brutal and coarse beast.

Ada Lawrence, *Young Lorenzo: Early life of D. H. Lawrence*, p. 25)

This description comes from Ada Lawrence, the writer's sister. It points at the bitterness that grew up between the parents, part of which becomes fictionalized and presented in great depth in *Sons and Lovers* (see Chapter 3). In contrast to his wife, Arthur Lawrence was virtually illiterate. He could just about manage to read the local newspapers. He spoke in a strong Midlands dialect, which Lydia disapproved of. D.H. Lawrence grew up to speak both standard English and dialect. He was to use the latter to great literary effect in his novels, poetry and plays. In *Sons and Lovers*, for instance, it was to become a symbol of coarseness and ignorance, embodied in the father figure in the novel. In his last novel, *Lady Chatterley's Lover*, the central character, Mellors, uses it to distinguish himself from the corrupt and spent upper-class Englishmen he sees about him and, as elsewhere, to express homely tenderness. Strong dialect is used by Lawrence in his novels and poetry at different stages in his career to perform different functions, to convey different meanings. The mining community also gave Lawrence material for his plays, such as *The Collier's Friday Night* and *The Widowing of Mrs Holroyd*.

A view of Nottingham and its agricultural environs, made at about the time of Lawrence's birth. The industrial sprawl of the city abuts sharply on to the green fields and meadows of 'the old agricultural England'.

The scenery of the industrial Midlands in the last quarter of the nineteenth century was one of contrasts. The rolling agricultural landscape ran right up to the great ash pits that came from the mines. The mining villages were ugly and the housing crowded, but not far from the front doors of the working people were the homes of the farmers and the cottages of the farm labourers, laid out amongst fields and streams. Lawrence called it 'the country of my heart' and in later life, having travelled extensively in other countries, remembered with

Lawrence despised the creeping industrialization of the Midlands. He saw it as a threat and a betrayal of the human spirit. It was associated in his mind with ugliness, which was to him 'the real tragedy of England'.

great feeling the contours and colours of Nottinghamshire and Derbyshire that formed his horizons for
the early years of his life. He was to return again and
again in prose and poetry to the places and people that
he had come to know in his youth, and the views he
knew 'better than any in the world'. For him it was 'the
old England', and this he related in his own mind to
past great writers, such as Wordsworth, who had drawn
their subjects, strength and nourishment from the rural
scene. He was to come to hate the industrial degradation

of the landscape, which, because of where he was born and at what stage of English industrial history, was so poignant and deep-felt. He had inherited a critical response to industrialization from certain great Victorian writers (Thomas Carlyle and John Ruskin, for example). He saw it, as they did, in terms not only of its effects on the landscape, but upon people themselves. The miners he grew up amongst were part of an ever increasing urban industrial working class. In later life he spoke strongly on the effects of industry on human beings:

> The real tragedy of England, as I see it, is the tragedy of ugliness. The country is so lovely: the man-made England is so vile . . . It was ugliness that betrayed the spirit of man in the nineteenth century. The great crime which the moneyed classes and promoters of industry committed in the palmy Victorian days was the condemning of the workers to ugliness, ugliness, ugliness.

This, he felt, caused in many the 'utter death of the human intuitive faculty', killing off the emotions and the capacity to respond to natural beauty and the loveliness in other human beings.

> When pure mechanization or materialism sets in . . . the most diverse of creatures fall into a common mechanical union.

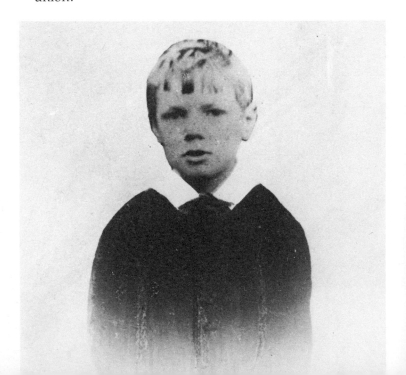

Lawrence as a small boy. He was 'a pale-faced, dirty-nosed, frail boy', and naturally gravitated towards the gentle world of his mother rather than the robust life of his father.

His attacks on industrialization and mechanization become a common theme in his writing, as will be seen. It is enough here to show how his resentment stems from very real contact with these deadening processes from his earliest days.

Lawrence was the fourth of five children born to Lydia and Arthur. He was to develop a disquieting closeness to his mother. Early in her marriage she had become disappointed and frustrated in love. Beyond a physical attraction, the parents had little in common. Lydia came to seek in her sons some of what was missing from her marriage.

> My mother was a clever, ironical, delicately moulded woman, of good, old burgher descent. She married below her. My father was dark, ruddy, with a fine laugh. . . . Their married life has been one carnal, bloody fight. I was born hating my father . . . This has been a kind of bond between me and my mother. We have loved each other, almost with a husband and wife love . . . we knew each other by instinct . . . We have been like one, so sensitive to each other that we never needed words. It has been rather terrible, and has made me, in some respects, abnormal.

A school photograph of Lawrence taken in 1894 when he was nine years old. His school at this time was Beauvale.

13

Lawrence went to Nottingham University College in 1906. This photograph of the students and staff was probably taken a year later. Lawrence is standing in the second-to-back row on the right. Also in the picture are Ernest Weekley (second row, 4th from the right) and Louie Burrows (bottom right).

It is easy to see why a sensitive child like Lawrence would instinctively side with his mother. She was a forceful woman, and came to stand for the powers of education and advancement. She could not instill in her husband the need to get on (he was too 'sanguine' and content with his lot) but she could keep her sons out of the mines and urge them on to a better life, something that in her eyes she could be proud of. She fought to keep them at school and to ensure that they had office jobs rather than following their father down the pits.

Lawrence was unsuited from the outset for the robust, physical life of the pits: 'I was a delicate, pale brat with a snuffy nose, whom most people treated quite gently as just an ordinary delicate lad.' In 1901 at the age of 16, he fell seriously ill with pneumonia. This was the first of many bouts of this debilitating illness that he was to suffer in his life. It was an illness that Lawrence realized 'damaged my health for life'. A close friend wrote of him after his death that his life was 'one long convalescence'. It left him weak with poor lungs. At the point of succumbing to the illness, he had been working for three months as a junior clerk at a factory in Nottingham making surgical appliances. He had come to the factory after leaving the Nottingham High School. This factory appears, as does so much autobiographical detail, in *Sons and Lovers*, Lawrence's great novel about the Midlands that he knew as a child and young man.

He could not go back to work. It took his mother many months to nurse her son back to health. Then, in 1902, he found a position as a pupil-teacher at the British School in Eastwood. He was untrained and found his first months exhausting and unrewarding. However, in 1903 a system was instigated whereby teachers could attend classes at a teacher-training centre set up in nearby Ilkeston. Lawrence went, with several of his friends. They set up an informal literary club, known as 'The Pagans'. Lawrence at this time was reading widely and deeply into English and European classics, including Shakespeare, Fielding, Dickens, George Eliot, Blake, Tennyson, Tolstoy, Ibsen, Maupassant and Victor Hugo. There has until relatively recently been a myth that Lawrence was basically ill-educated and ignorant of the great tradition of literature. A glance at this list, which is not exhaustive, shows this to be a completely false assumption. The Pagans also discussed politics and philosophy, all of which went to help the young Lawrence formulate his own beliefs and passions.

He was to remain a pupil-teacher until 1906, when he took up a place at Nottingham University College to read for a degree. It was at this time that he started to experiment with his own writing. In 1905 he had composed his first poems and the following year he embarked upon what was to become his first novel, *The White Peacock*.

A photograph taken of Lawrence on his 21st birthday in 1906. It was in this year that he was to start writing The White Peacock.

15

Lawrence has left us a résumé of these years leading up to his first published poems, the moment at which he was launched upon his writing career (though the actual decision to give up teaching and become a professional writer was to wait a few years):

I was glad to leave college. It had meant mere disillusion, instead of the living contact of men. From college I went down to Croydon, near London, to teach in a new elementary school . . . It was while I was at Croydon, when I was twenty-three, that the girl who had been the chief friend of my youth . . . copied some of my poems, and without telling me, sent them to the *English Review*, which had just had a glorious rebirth under Ford Madox Hueffer.

Hueffer was most kind. He printed the poems, and asked me to come and see him. The girl had launched me, so easily, on my literary career, like a princess cutting a thread, launching a ship.

In 1908 Lawrence went to teach at the Davidson Road Boy's School, in Croydon. He disliked 'teaching and trying to tame some fifty or sixty malicious young human animals'.

Lawrence's 'chief friend' of his youth was a girl called Jessie Chambers. Apart from his mother, Jessie was to be the biggest influence on his early development, and not only because she sent the fateful poems to an influential literary journal. Their relationship is described in fictionalized form in *Sons and Lovers*. She was brought up on a farm about two miles from Eastwood. Lawrence first met her in 1901, while he was working at the factory.

Jessie Chambers at the age of 23. She was one of the most important early influences on the development of the young writer. She is portrayed as Miriam in Sons and Lovers.

He quickly struck up an intense friendship with her. They read together and he taught her French. With her, he experienced the pains of first love and explored an entirely new emotional and spiritual world. Many of his early poems are written to her or about her.

Of those first poems ('Campions' and 'Guelder Roses', for example) he was to note in later life:

> Any young lady might have written them and been pleased with them: as I was pleased with them. But it was after that, when I was twenty, that my real demon would now and then get hold of me and shake more real poems out of me, making me uneasy.

> *(The Complete Poems of D. H. Lawrence*, p. 23)

The earliest pieces are derivative and unformed. Their lack of originality stems in part from Lawrence's inexperience. They are in rhyme, which he was later to reject in favour of his own form of free verse (verse with neither a rhyme scheme nor a formal metrical pattern – see Chapter 6).

Lawrence was briefly to engage himself to Jessie. But along with the agonies of first love went a curious antagonism on his part towards the girl. 'Look, you are a nun, I give you what I would give a holy nun. So you must let me marry a woman I can kiss and embrace and make the mother of my children.' They were both 'fiercely virgin' and curiously unable to make the leap into full physical love with each other. Lawrence, to some extent unfairly, gives Jessie the sole responsibility for the impasse at which their relationship arrives. The letter to her signals the end of an important relationship: a relationship that Lawrence was to use again and again as material for his creative work. Lawrence was experimenting with poems, short stories and the novel up until 1912, when he left teaching in Croydon for good. His mother had died the previous year, after an illness that had left her in agony. Lawrence nursed her until she died, an experience that almost broke him.

> Then . . . for me, everything collapsed, save the mystery of death, and the haunting of death in life. I was twenty-five, and from the death of my mother, the world began to dissolve around me, beautiful, iridescent, but passing away substanceless. Till I almost dissolved myself, and was very ill: when I was twenty-six. Then slowly the world came back: or I returned: but to another world.
>
> (*Phoenix: The Posthumous Papers of D. H. Lawrence*, p. 253)

With the death of his mother went the strength of her immediate hold over him. To some extent it is true that while she was still alive, he could not enter fully into a relationship with another woman: so great and so complex was the bond between mother and son.

It is no simple coincidence that within a year he had met the woman with whom he was to spend the rest of his life. This woman was Frieda Weekly, then married to the Professor of French at Nottingham University,

Ernest Weekly. She was the daughter of a German aristocrat, Baron von Richthofen. Lawrence had gone to Professor Weekly in an attempt to secure a teaching position at a German university. Frieda has a vivid account of her first sight of the young Lawrence:

It was an April day in 1912. He came for lunch, to see my husband about a lectureship at a German university. Lawrence was also at a critical period of his life just then. The death of his mother had shaken the foundations of his health for a second time. He had given up his post as a schoolmaster at Croydon. He had done with his past life.

Lawrence and Frieda in 1914, the year they married, with John Middleton Murry. This was one of his most creative and positive periods. He was working on The Rainbow *while the threat of war hung over Europe.*

She goes on to say that,

> I see him before me as he entered the house. A long, thin figure, quick straight legs, light, sure movements. He seemed so obviously simple. Yet he arrested my attention. There was something more than met the eye . . . After leaving that night . . . he wrote to me: 'You are the most wonderful woman in England.'

(Frieda Lawrence,
'Not I, But the Wind. . .', p. 22)

Frieda at the time of their meeting had been married twelve years and was the mother of three children. Lawrence was to take her away from her comfortable middle-class life to spend the next 18 years of their time together wandering the world, making their home in Italy, Australia, New Mexico and only intermittently returning to England.

Frieda's marriage to Weekly had left her emotionally unfulfilled. Lawrence recognized in her a veiled vitality and passion. He wrote to a friend, Edward Garnett (then editor of the *Century* and successor to Ford Madox Hueffer as Lawrence's champion in the world of publishing): ' . . . she's the finest woman I've ever met . . . she's splendid, she really is.' They met frequently and finally decided to go away together, first to her home country, Germany.

Frieda and Lawrence lived in this house, called Mountain Cottage, in Derbyshire through part of 1918 and 1919, just prior to their leaving England virtually for good.

He seemed to have lifted me body and soul out of all my past life. This young man of twenty-six had taken all my fate, all my destiny, into his hands. And we had known each other barely for six weeks.

('Not I, But the Wind. . .')

They went from Germany into Italy on foot, walking over the Alps. He had given up the idea of applying for a lectureship. Indeed, in the bliss of his new-found relationship, he was to enter into one of his most creative periods. During this period, which lasted until the early years of the First World War (around 1915) he was to complete his first great novel, *Sons and Lovers*, finish a collection of poems charting the course of his relationship with Frieda (by no means a smooth one), called, *Look! We Have Come Through!*, embark upon a new novel, initially called 'The Sisters' (but published as two separate though connected novels, *The Rainbow* and *Women in Love*) and write many short stories of great power.

In 1913 he fell seriously ill once more. Frieda and he had returned to England. While staying with Edward Garnett in Kent, Lawrence had remarked to a fellow guest while holding his chest, 'I've something here, savage, that is heavier than concrete. If I don't get it out it will kill me.' It would be many years before the killer disease turberculosis was diagnosed.

In 1916 and 1917 the Lawrences were in Cornwall, living near a place called Zennor. Lawrence liked the 'rough sea and this bare country, King Arthur's country,' but it was no real compensation for the gloom he felt about the War.

The First World War shattered Lawrence's faith in humanity. He suffered personally: while staying in Cornwall, he and Frieda came under suspicion of being German spies (because of her background) and on several occasions he had to suffer the ignominy of undergoing a medical test to see if he was fit for active service. His creative genius changed under the influence of these experiences. Much of his writing after this period becomes more pessimistic, darker in its dealings with human destiny. This is most noticeable in the change that came about between his writing *The Rainbow* and its more difficult sequel, *Women in Love*. In a fine letter to Lady Ottoline Morrell he wrote:

> I feel sometimes I shall go mad, because there is nowhere to go, no 'new world' . . . I almost wish I could go to the war – not to shoot: I have vowed an eternal oath that I won't shoot in this war, not even if I am shot . . . . The death of Rupert Brooke fills me more and more with the sense of the fatuity of it all . . . O God. O God, it is all too much of a piece: it is like madness . . . It isn't my disordered imagination. There is a wagtail sitting on the gate-post. I see how sweet and swift heaven is. But hell is slow and creeping and viscous and insect-teeming: as is this Europe now, this England.

(Moore (ed.) *The collected letters of D. H. Lawrence*, pp 337–8)

Lawrence first met Lady Ottoline Morrell in 1914 and was to visit her at Garsington, her country home in Oxfordshire. Here he met many important and influential people, like the philosopher, Bertrand Russell, with whom Lady Ottoline was having an affair.

23

He felt that he wanted to escape the madness in Europe. He formulated a plan to go with a few close friends to a faraway country and there set up an ideal society, free from materialism and war, where each individual could develop to their own potential. He called this utopia *Rananim*. It had literary connections with earlier nineteenth-century idealist schemes, such as the Romantic poet, Samuel Taylor Coleridge's plan to construct in the New World (North America) an ideal society called *Pantisocracy*. Lawrence never succeeded in setting up his commune, but he managed to flee England, virtually

A sketch by Lawrence of David Garnett, a novelist and critic and member of the Bloomsbury set.

for good, to embark upon what he called his 'savage pilgrimage'. This was in 1919, a year after the First World War finished. 'I can't tell you how glad I am to be out of England', he wrote to Edward Garnett. 'I feel as if not once, all the time I was in England, had I really wakened up.'

He had also been crushed by the English censor's decision to proclaim *The Rainbow* an obscene book. It had been published in 1915, and was suppressed within months. This was the start of Lawrence's battles with the censor, which were to continue all his life. A major subject in his writing was the relationships between men and women. This obviously included the topic of sexual relations, a matter on which he wrote in detail with great sensitivity, with 'terrifying honesty'.

In 1923 the Lawrences went to Mexico. They visited the pre-Aztec Pyramid of the Sun at Teotihuacan. Here Lawrence got his ideas for the novel, The Plumed Serpent, *which he began in this year.*

25

Lawrence at Santa Fe, in New Mexico, outside the house of his friend Witter Bynner.

Opposite *The Flying Heart Ranch at San Cristobel, New Mexico, given to Frieda by Mabel Dodge in 1924, in return for the manuscript of* Sons and Lovers. *When Lawrence moved in, he changed its name to 'Lobo'.*

From England he was to go with Frieda to Italy, Sicily, Sardinia, Ceylon (Sri Lanka), Australia, California, New Mexico and Mexico. He sought constantly to put himself in contact with primitive centres of powerful life sources that were not those of modern decadent Europe. His

unconventional, but serious and deeply-felt outlook led him to search for an alternative to the madness and corruption he had left behind. He sought constantly in his writing to explore new relationships for men and women with the natural world about them. There is a great deal of the Old Testament prophet about him (he is reminiscent of the Romantic poet, William Blake in this respect) and his preaching often intrudes into his fiction.

In 1924, he was diagnosed as having tuberculosis of the lungs. In 1925 he returned to live permanently in Europe. He was now established as a writer. Apart from his poems and novels, he had published several travel books (*Sea and Sardinia* and *Mornings in Mexico*, for example), some works of criticism (*A Study of Thomas Hardy*, *Studies in Classic American Literature*) and some philosophical tracts dealing mainly with the implications of Freud's writings on the unconscious, an area that fascinated Lawrence, and which in many respects illuminates or complements his explorations into the darker sides of human nature and human motivation.

In spite of his reputation, he remained poor most of his life. He was continually at odds with the authorities. In 1929, some of his paintings were exhibited in London. They were seized by the police for being obscene; the manuscript of a collection of poems (*Pansies*) was impounded at customs. Perhaps the most notorious episode was the scandal surrounding his last novel, *Lady Chatterley's Lover*. It was first published in Italy in 1928. A full version was not published in England until 1960. In the introduction to this edition, the opening sentence reads, '*Lady Chatterley's Lover* is not a dirty book. It is clean and serious and beautiful.' It took the censors over thirty years to see this. This is a measure of how misunderstood Lawrence was in his lifetime, and indeed for many years after his death. He died in 1930 in a sanatorium in Southern France. His wife Frieda left the best epitaph in a letter to a friend:

Opposite The Lawrence family grave in Eastwood churchyard, Nottinghamshire. Lawrence was diagnosed as having tuberculosis in 1924 and died of the disease six years later.

What he had seen and felt and known he gave in his writing to his fellow men, the splendour of living, the hope of more and more life he had given them, a heroic and immeasurable gift.

(Frieda Lawrence,
The Memoirs and Correspondence, p. 106)

2 The Making of a Writer

Opposite A sketch by Lawrence of the ranch in New Mexico made to accompany a letter to his niece, Margaret Needham.

D.H. Lawrence has been considered by many to be the most important novelist in England writing in the first half of the twentieth century. Henry James thought him one of the four best writers of his generation. He started his writing career in the manner of the great Victorian novelists, such as George Eliot and Thomas Hardy. That is, in *Sons and Lovers* and other early writings, his manner is basically realistic: his characters express themselves through their actions. Other techniques such as significant imagery or symbolic scenes enable him to look into the hearts and minds of his characters, revealing powerful emotions and feelings that are not simply expressed in action. But generally speaking with this novel he sticks to the well-worn paths of the English literary tradition. It is with *The Rainbow* and *Women in Love* that his break with nineteenth-century realism occurs. Just how important and innovative these novels are will be discussed later. It is important to register here that Lawrence was essentially experimental, at least in his full-length novels (as opposed to the short stories); that he found he had things to say about human life and relations that no other novelist had said and that he sought for new ways in which to express them.

corral

little barn

to spring

Friedas cabin

slope up to mount

barn

2 room cabin

F. room (sitting room)

porch over kitchen door

shed

oven

slope down to desert & Rio Grande

alfalfa field.

We have only one little spring of water – pure water – that will fill
a pail in about 3 minutes: it runs the same summer & winter. If we want to
grow anything, we must water, irrigate. Mabel used to bring the water in a
made ditch, over deep places by a wooden runnel bridges, for nearly 3 miles: from the
Gallina Canyon. Then, from the home canyon, he brought it down two miles. It's very difficult,
though, in a dry country with dry gravelly soil. You can't bring much flow, so far: & in
summer very often none. So we leave the ranch quite wild – only there's abundant feed
for the five horses. And if we wanted to take the trouble, we could bring the water here as
Mabel did, & have a little farm. – There's quite a lot of land, really – it say 160 acres,
but it takes a terrible long time to go round the fence, through the wild forest. – We
got lots of wild strawberries – & we still get gallons of wild raspberries, up our own little
canyon, where no soul ever goes. If we ride two miles, we can go no further. Beyond,
all savage, unbroken mountains.
    We get our things from Taos – 17 miles – either by wagon or when someone
is coming in a car. Our road is no road – a breaking through the forest – but people come
to see us. Every evening, just after tea, we saddle up and ride down to Del Monte Ranch,
for the milk, butter, eggs, & letters. The old trail passes this gate, & the mailman, on horseback,
leaves all the mail in a box nailed on a tree. Usually we get back just at dark. Yesterday
we rode down to San Cristobal, where there is a cross-roads, a blacksmith, & a tiny village
with no shop, no anything, save the blacksmith – only a handful of Mexicans who speak Spanish.
We went to get Frieda's grey horse – the Azul – shod. They call him in Spanish el Azul –
the Blue. – During the day there's always plenty to do – chopping wood, carrying

Lawrence and Aldous Huxley, novelist and essayist, at the Villa Mirenda in Italy, 1926. Lawrence had met Huxley in London and their friendship flourished in Tuscany.

His literary career (spanning some twenty or so years up to his death in 1930) can be seen as a series of changes, of shedding past thoughts and obsessions in his work and moving on to new areas of exploration. Of course, there are themes that run consistently throughout (for instance, the deadening effects of industrialization on human growth and potential; the need to get beyond purely mental life into a realm of feeling and spontaneity, associated with the natural world – its opposite being the socially constructed world of people). But with each major novel (*Sons and Lovers* (1913), *The Rainbow* (1915), *Women in Love* (1920), *Aaron's Rod* (1922), *Kangaroo* (1925), *The Plumed Serpent* (1926), *Lady Chatterley's Lover* (1928) Lawrence was concerned to explore new territory. *Sons and Lovers* is one of the greatest novels written about the English working class. It is, among other things, a direct descendent of the Victorian social novel. It is a long way removed in tone, style and content from *The Plumed Serpent*, for instance, which moves to an exotic land to explore among the Aztecs of Mexico the wisdom of a past civilization set against the corruption of western twentieth-century values.

Lawrence travelled widely and each new place inspired him to write in a new manner about new aspects of the human condition. He had come a long way from his essentially working-class, provincial English upbringing. Being a writer, these transitions are recorded in his fiction. He tried to move beyond class, putting himself consciously outside society in order to be able to look in and analyse and write about what he saw.

Lawrence was one of the most personal of writers. Therefore each of his novels has a complex but direct relation with the situation and place in which he found himself. They draw consistently from the people and experiences of the moment, to varying degrees. He believed passionately in the spontaneous nature of his art. He repeats time and again that it is not his aim to capture and constrict life and thought and feeling in his works, but to record their passing, their movement in transit, as it were, from one state to another. He was not the sort of artist who crafts his work into a state of near perfection. He always believed that the utterance would give shape to itself. In a preface he was to write for his *Collected Poems* (1928) he states:

> It seems to me that no poetry, not even the best, should be judged as if it existed in the absolute, in the vacuum of the absolute. Even the best poetry, when it is at all personal, needs the penumbra of its own time and place and circumstance to make it full and whole.

'Think I'll turn into a painter, it costs less, and probably would pay better than writing.' In 1924, Lawrence turned his attention more seriously to painting.

This is true for all Lawrence's work, though here it is applied only to his poetry. He says elsewhere, in a letter, that:

> I want to write live things, if crude and half formed, rather than beautiful dying decadent things with sad odours.
>
> (letter, 1909)

Lawrence is taking a swipe here at the decadent literature being written in France and England at the end of the nineteenth century. But he is also positively stating his own case, he is stating his own way of crafting his work.

In the brief twenty or so years of his working life, apart from the novels, Lawrence was to write many short stories, poems, plays, essays, works of literary criticism, reviews, travel books and many letters to his friends and literary acquaintances. He was also to become an extremely accomplished painter. This prolific output varies considerably in quality. This is to some extent inevitable, given his belief in writing spontaneously. He also did not believe in revising and checking his work, though he would on occasion completely rework certain sections.

His work has affected many people profoundly. This is as true today as it was when he was writing. Lawrence is the sort of writer who commands violent reactions, either of admiration or of dislike. Either way it is difficult to remain untouched by the force of his fiction and not to feel the passion and commitment with which he approached his work. 'He was a part of me: he had entered into my veins at a very vulnerable moment, of adolescence, changing into maturity.' These are the words of the historian, A. L. Rowse.

Another record, this time of Lawrence the man, has been left us by the philosopher and mathematician, Bertrand Russell. Lawrence first met him in 1915. Russell was to say of him,

> He is amazing; he sees through and through one. He is infallible. He is like Ezekiel or some other Old Testament prophet, prophesying. Of course, the blood of his nonconformist preaching ancestors is strong in him, but he sees everything and is always right.

35

Bertrand Russell (1872-1970), known mainly for his philosophical and mathematical works. Lawrence first met him through Lady Ottoline Morrell and later planned a lecture tour with him. Lawrence satirizes the Cambridge intellectual in Women in Love *in the figure of Sir Josiah Mattheson.*

This is an astute judgement and apt for several reasons. The notion of Lawrence the prophet railing against a corrupt modern society and foretelling its doom is a common one. *Women in Love*, for instance, is a novel littered with prophetic statements (usually coming from Rupert Birkin, Lawrence's *alter ego*) about the world. Birkin's solution is to seek a 'perfect union with a woman – sort of ultimate marriage – and there isn't anything else.' There are many examples of Lawrence preaching about the evils of society. The contemporary novelist, E.M. Forster, took exception to this quality in Lawrence, and wrote to him saying,

> I like the Lawrence . . . who sees birds and is physically restful and wrote *The White Peacock* . . . but I do not like the deaf impercipient fanatic who . . . believes that there is no other part for others to take: he sometimes interests and sometimes frightens and angers me . . .

Many critics see Lawrence's preaching in some of his works, especially the novels, to be a flaw, an area of artistic failure.

Lawrence was brought up in the Congregational Church. Of all novelists of this century, he shows the most profound and thorough knowledge of the Bible.

> I was brought up on the Bible, and seem to have it in my bones. From early childhood I have been familiar with Apocalyptic language and Apocalyptic image: not because I spent my time reading Revelation, but because I was sent to Sunday School and to Chapel . . . and was always having the Bible read to me.

The Chapel was a social as well as a spiritual institution. It was a focal point for the community. Lawrence's mother befriended the clergyman in Eastwood, the Revd Robert Reid. He was educated and was an outlet for Lydia Lawrence's intellectual aspirations. He founded a literary society which Lawrence attended, while still at school. He was one of the first channels by which Lawrence came into contact with the wider world of literature and the arts.

Inside the Congregational Church in Eastwood. One of Lawrence's first contacts with the world of literature and the imagination was through the Church and more especially through the minister, the Reverend Robert Reid.

Lawrence rejected Christianity. He did not believe that it could provide for the salvation of modern man. But he did retain a religious feeling, translated into other areas and taking different precepts. He believed in a world beyond the materialistic. He believed that part of his function as a writer was to find out the way towards salvation for his generation.

> The essential function of art is moral. Not aesthetic, not decorative, not pastime and recreation, but moral.

This shows the prophet in the man. It is part of his power and uniqueness, his strength as a personality and writer; it is also the seat of his weakness, because of his tendency to become fanatical and dogmatic.

> . . . and my novels must be written from the depth of my religious experience. That I must keep to because I can only work like that. And my Cockneyism and commoness are only when the deep feeling doesn't find its way out, and a sort of jeer comes instead, and sentimentality, and purpulism.

(letter to Edward Garnett, 1914)

The Church thus gave him a religious framework which he never lost (though he shed orthodox Christianity). It also gave him access to a powerful rhythmic language (that of the Authorized Version of the Bible) which he uses to great effect in his fiction. And finally in the form of the Revd Robert Reid, it provided the means by which he came into contact with the world of literature. In Eastwood, this world was also made accessible by the Mechanics' Institute Library, a repository of great books that Lawrence, coming from the background that he did, might otherwise have found difficult to obtain.

Jessie Chambers, the young woman from Haggs Farm also helped shape the young man. With Jessie he embarked upon what he called 'thought adventures'. With her he went far beyond the readings of the literary society. And she imbued everything they read with a special significance.

The farm was in itself a place also vested with significance. 'Whatever I forget, I shall never forget the Haggs – I loved it so . . . it really was new life began in me

Opposite Haggs Farm, where the Chambers family lived. It was situated only a few miles from Eastwood, and the young Lawrence was frequently to visit Jessie there. However, he came to love the farm for its own sake. He wrote, two years before his death that, 'Whatever else I am, I am somewhere still the same Bert who rushed with such joy to the Haggs'.

there.' He associates it with the 'old agricultural England of Shakespeare and Milton and Fielding and George Eliot.' The farm was only a few miles from the squalor of Eastwood, and he often treats it like an Arcadian retreat, a place to which he can escape into quiet and another world. He depicts the life that goes on there with great sensitivity and colour in *Sons and Lovers*. This contact with the land remained an important part of his life. It also brought him contentment of a sort in the form of simple physical tasks, in which he took a great deal of delight.

3 Sons and Lovers

Sons and Lovers was Lawrence's third novel, started in 1910 when he was twenty-five, and published two years later. It is considered by many critics to be a landmark in the history of the English novel. It is the first novel that takes as its subject matter the English working class, written from the point of view of one of its members: Lawrence, as we know, was the son of a miner. *Sons and Lovers* describes in very fine detail his experiences as a child and young man in fictionalized form. It is a novel that stands in the divide between the nineteenth and twentieth centuries. In terms of literary history, the book looks back to the nineteenth century realist mode, deriving much of its strength and colour from its powerful descriptive passages; and forward to the 'psychological' approach of the Modernist writers, such as Joyce and T.S. Eliot. Lawrence was to write the bulk of it while still being very close to his subject matter. He left England with Frieda in 1912 and finished the novel in Italy. But it remains a novel about a Midlands mining community written by someone who knew the world intimately and what is more, really knew no other at the time of writing.

It ranks in its portrayal of life, character and environment with the works of great Victorian writers like Charles Dickens, George Eliot and Elizabeth Gaskell. But Lawrence also wanted to get below the surface of external events to show the inner lives of his characters,

Opposite Frieda and Lawrence in Italy at the Villa Mirenda. Italy was a country that continually inspired Lawrence in his work and gave him the right sort of environment in which he could create. He was to work on Sons and Lovers *during his first trip there in 1912.*

Moorgreen colliery, near Eastwood, which in Sons and Lovers *becomes Minton Mine, just as Moorgreen Reservoir becomes Nethermere and Willey Water. Lawrence drew on the familiar landmarks of his youth heavily in this early novel.*

'the ebb and flow' of their sympathies. The greatness of *Sons and Lovers* lies in part in the combined strengths of these two approaches.

> The novels and poems come unwatched from one's pen. And then the absolute need one has for some sort of satisfactory mental attitude towards oneself and things in general makes one try to abstract some definite conclusions from one's experience.

Lawrence wrote this many years after *Sons and Lovers* (in *Fantasia*). But it is a statement very applicable to that novel. All his working life Lawrence used his personal experience of the world and people that he knew as the raw material for his fiction. In *Sons and Lovers* this drawing on life is more obvious and sustained than in any other piece of his major fiction. However, it is not autobiographical in any simple way. Lawrence himself was well aware of the complex relationship between life and art. He was to write to Jessie Chambers, who in the novel appears as Miriam, concerning the early drafts of *Sons and Lovers*: 'Of course it isn't the truth. It isn't meant for the truth. It's an adaptation from life, as all art must be.'

Real life is the raw material that Lawrence uses. It is his point of departure into the realm of fiction. In *Sons and Lovers* he was to remain very close to that real life, to people and places and circumstances. He has left a very lucid account of the plot which is worth quoting in full, because it sums up the external events and psychological motives of the major characters:

> A woman of character and refinement goes into the lower class, and has no satisfaction in her own life. She has had a passion for her husband, so the children are born of passion, and have heaps of vitality. But as her sons grow up, she selects them as lovers – first the eldest, then the second. These sons are *urged* into life by their reciprocal love of their mother – urged on and on. But when they come to manhood, they can't love, because their mother is the strongest power in their lives, and holds them . . . As soon as the young men come into contact with women there is a split. William gives his sex to a fribble, and his mother holds his soul. But the split kills him, because he doesn't know where he is. The next son gets a woman who fights for his soul – fights his mother. The son loves the mother – all the sons hate and are jealous of the father. The battle goes on between the mother and the girl, with the son as object. The mother gradually proves the stronger, because of the tie of blood. The son decides to leave his soul in his mother's hands, and, like his elder brother, go for passion. Then the split begins to tell again. But, almost unconsciously, the mother realises what is the matter and begins to die. The son casts off his mistress, attends to his mother dying. He is left in the end naked of everything, with the drift towards death.

The central characters are mentioned – Paul Morel (the hero of the book in whom Lawrence invests much of his own feelings and life), Mrs Morel, his mother, Miriam Leivers, the girl from the farm, who 'fights' the mother for the soul of Paul, William the elder brother, who dies young, and finally Clara Dawes, the 'mistress' he 'casts off', an older woman separated from her husband, and with whom Paul has his first full sexual experience. They are all drawn from people that Lawrence knew as he grew up in Eastwood. In the novel, he is reliving recently passed and deeply felt experience 'to abstract some definite conclusions.' It is important to recognize this fact when reading the novel, but it does not change the power of the novel itself, the 'art' which transforms it into fiction.

The outline above also reveals, in a way the novel itself does not, the psychological force and pressure behind the main action. In other words, the novel does not spell out, but rather puts before the reader in the form of developed characterization and situations, the intense flow of emotional, sexual and psychological life, that underpins the ordinary life.

The market place in Eastwood. Lawrence renamed his home town in Sons and Lovers, *calling it* Bestwood. *It is here that the young Paul Morel grows up, invested with the memories of the author.*

The book is divided into two parts. The first sets out the life of the Midlands mining community that Lawrence knew intimately. We can feel in his descriptions of the Nottingham countryside, the small mining villages, the miners' cramped but clean cottages and the forms of the people themselves, with their thick Midlands dialect, and ill-educated but vital and passionate outlook on life, the great sympathy and understanding he had for them. He brings before the reader ordinary life and paints it in a special light that lends it power and uniqueness. Jessie Chambers once said of Lawrence that:

> It was his power to transmute the common experience into significance that I always felt to be Lawrence's greatest gift. He did not distinguish between small and great happenings; the common round was full of mystery, awaiting interpretation. Born and bred of working people, he had the rare gift of seeing them from within.

Many rows of miners' cottages were built in the nineteenth century to accommodate the swelling numbers of workers. They were in the main ugly and cramped.

Sons and Lovers is in part about this 'common round'. It is about the life inside one of the miners' cottages, that of the Morel family, and the rhythms of their life: the children, fairs, baking bread, squabbling over the money that the father earns down the pit.

Opposite
Nottingham Goose Fair as it was around the time of Lawrence's birth. It was an occasion of great festivity and excitement.

> When he was nineteen, he was earning only twenty shillings a week, but he was happy. His painting went well, and life went well enough. On the Good Friday he organized a walk to the Hemlock Stone. There were three lads of his own age, then Annie and Arthur, Miriam and Geoffrey . . . Morel, as usual, was up early, whistling and sawing in the yard. At seven o'clock the family heard him buy threepenny-worth of hot-cross buns; he talked with gusto to the little girl who brought them . . . He turned away several boys who came with more buns, telling them they had been 'kested' by a little lass. Then Mrs Morel got up, and the family straggled down. It was an immense luxury to everybody, this lying in bed just beyond the ordinary time on a weekday. And Paul and Arthur read before breakfast, and had the meal unwashed, sitting in their shirt-sleeves. This was another holiday luxury. The room was warm. Everything felt free of care and anxiety. There was a sense of plenty in the house.

In this passage we can see Lawrence's use of descriptive language. He paints a convincing picture of life. It is the attention that he pays to small detail that gives to the reader a sense of fully realized experience. Morel uses the Midlands dialect term, 'kested', which helps place him in his community and to reveal something about the man. We get a strong sense of family bonding and of a holiday atmosphere that has replaced the normal routine of a working day. The feeling of excitement and anticipation is skilfully and simply built up.

The first half of the novel dwells more on these superb evocations of the external lives of the family, the village and the pit. Only occasionally does Lawrence take us below the surface and point to another realm of existence, that of the psychic lives (and by psychic we mean internal, emotional lives of his characters). For example, the first chapter ends with a fight between Morel and his wife when the former comes home one evening drunk. She is pregnant with Paul at the time. He turns her out into the yard, where she stands cold and isolated from the world. Lawrence describes in prose of great beauty a feeling of power and mystery that comes upon her in her anguish as she senses the child within her womb.

> The moon was high and magnificent in the August night. Mrs Morel, seared with passion, shivered to find herself out there in a great white light, that fell cold on her, and gave a shock to her inflamed soul . . . She became aware of something about her. With an effort she roused herself to see what it was that penetrated her consciousness. The tall white lilies were reeling in the moonlight, and the air was charged with their perfume, as with a presence . . . she drank a deep draught of the scent. It almost made her dizzy.
>   Mrs Morel leaned on the garden gate, looking out, and she lost herself awhile. She did not know what she thought. Except for a slight feeling of sickness, and her consciousness in the child, herself melted out like scent into the shiny, pale air. After a time the child, too, melted with her in the mixing-pot of moonlight, and she rested with the hills and lilies and houses, all swum together in a kind of swoon.

This is a very different style of prose from the episode where the family prepare for their holiday. It is describing an intense experience, at once very private and larger than the character who experiences it. It is a mystical moment in which Mrs Morel transcends her immediate problems, and finds peace in the sensation of her unborn child, and in the overpowering scent of the lilies and strange cold light of the moon. Moon and lilies, we imagine, are actually there in the garden, but they also become potent symbols. They symbolize a world of nature that is indifferent to the small problems of people. The moon's light falls 'cold' on Mrs Morel. The lilies and the moon are nature shown in a cold, hard form, totally separated from human life. It is in part this realization that makes Mrs Morel 'dizzy' and 'swoon'. The mystery is also associated with the mystery of life itself. The child growing inside her contributes to her unconscious feelings. Both she and the child are finally overwhelmed by the surroundings, 'the hills and lilies and houses', and the obliteration of the human consciousness in her is complete. There is also a sense in which in her fight with Morel she is drawn closer to the child, although the child is not yet a separate entity. The central theme of the book is Paul's relationship with his mother and her influence upon his development, and in this light the scene is also of great importance. It is the first indication of a special bond between mother and son. A sense of irony is present in the episode when one remembers that Walter Morel is slumped in a drunken stupor in the house.

A scene from the film of Sons and Lovers *in which the miner, Walter, flies at his wife, Gertrude, in an act of drunken violence.*

The emotional separation of husband and wife also occurs in this chapter. She has come to realize that a miners' wife can expect only a life of drudgery and has accepted that.

The world seemed a dreamy place, where nothing else would happen for her . . . till the children grew up . . . . The father was serving beer in a public-house, swilling himself drunk. She despised him, and was tied to him.

(*Sons and Lovers*, p.12)

The Three Tuns public house, the model Lawrence used for the Moon and Stars in Sons and Lovers . *It appears in the opening chapter, where we see the respectable and responsible Mrs Morel passing it on her way home from the fair, knowing that her husband is inside drinking away their sparse money.*

In an act of 'masculine clumsiness' he cuts the curly hair of the eldest son, William. Mrs Morel is outraged, and comes to understand that her emotional life with him is over.

> . . . she knew, and Moral knew, that that act had caused something momentous to take place in her soul. She remembered the scene al her life, as one in which she had suffered most intensely.
>
> (*Sons and Lovers*, p.25)

William grows into a passionate young man. In many ways he is a more successful and considerate version of his father. He contracts a fever working in London and dies. It is interesting to note that in his account of the novel's progress, Lawrence describes William's death in terms of a psychological state rather than that of an actual physical illness. In the novel, the psychological nature of his illness (caused by an emotional rift in the man's soul brought about by the woman he marries and his mother's power over him) is not immediately obvious. In many ways, he is sacrificed to his mother's desire to see him get on in the world. Her husband has disappointed her:

> The pity was, she was too much his opposite. She could not be content with the little he might be: she would have him the much that he ought to be. So, in seeking to make him nobler than could be, she destroyed him.

After William's death, Mrs Morel pours her energies into the second son, Paul. He becomes seriously ill and is nursed back to health by her. His near death also brings her back into the land of the living. Almost losing a second son jolts her out of a state of morbid lethargy and depression. Paul proves an easier target for her domination. He is frailer, more sensitive and feels an instinctive affinity with her. She feels his dependence.

Lawrence's feelings about this mother and son relationship, based on his own experiences, found expression in other forms. At the time of writing the novel, he was also experimenting with poetry. In one of these poems, called 'Monologue of a Mother', he was imaginatively to put himself in her position and write with her voice about 'dead days fusing together in dross' and 'the long years of sitting in my husband's house'. The second verse has her speaking about her feelings for her son:

> Strange he is, my son, for whom I have waited like a
>   lover;
> Strange to me, like a captive in a foreign country,
>   haunting
> The confines, gazing out beyond, where the winds go
>   free;
> White and gaunt, with wistful eyes that hover
> Always on the distance . . .

MARKED PROOF

Which please return to Publisher.

Date Feb 21/13

Lawrence finished writing Sons and Lovers *in 1912, the year he eloped with Frieda Weekly. This is a page from the proofs, corrected by the author.*

The feeling expressed here is similar to that revealed in *Sons and Lovers*. The language that puts the mother and son in the role of lovers or husband and wife is repeated, in the later episodes of the novels, when Paul is a young man. On one occasion, for example, he takes her on an outing to Lincoln. She is old and frail-looking. He is trying to cheer her up. He has started work at the factory and has money to spend on her.

They ate a meal that she considered wildly extravagant. 'Don't imagine I like it,' she said, as she ate her cutlet. 'I *don't* like it, I really don't! Just *think* of your money wasted!' 'You never mind my money,' he said. 'You forget I'm a fellow taking his girl for an outing.'

The second part of the novel charts Paul's growth into
a young man. These chapters have at their centre Paul's
emerging consciousness and sexuality. Lawrence
explores the tremendous tensions and emotional turmoil
in Paul, brought about by the unbearable demands being
put upon him by his mother, at a time when he is drawn
to girls of his own age.

His first real love is Miriam Leivers. She is shown
from the outset to be a threat to the mother because she
appeals to the intellectual and spiritual side of Paul's
nature, an area that the mother holds as her own. When
Paul experiences full sexual passion with Clara Dawes,
Mrs Morel feels less threatened. This is an area of her
son's life in which he must go to other women to find
fulfilment. She can accept this. There are many scenes
developing the theme of Paul's divided loyalties. He
often stays out late, at the farm where Miriam lives. He
finds consolation on the farm not only from Miriam but
also from the rural farming community.

At one point Paul confesses to his mother that he does
not love Miriam. His mother's reaction reveals her fears
about this girl:

'No, Mother – I really don't love her. I talk to her, but
I want to come home to you.'
'I can't bear it. I could let another woman – but not her
– she'd leave me no room, not a bit of room . . .'
And immediately he hated Miriam bitterly.
'And I've never – you know, Paul – I've never had a
husband – not really.'
He stroked his mother's hair, and his mouth was on her
throat.
'And she exults so in taking you from me – she's not
like ordinary girls.'
'Well, I don't love her, Mother,' he murmured, bowing
his head and hiding his eyes on her shoulder in misery.
His mother kissed him a long, fervent kiss.
'My boy!' she said, in a voice trembling with passionate
love.
'There' said his Mother, 'now go to bed . . . There's your
father – now go.' Suddenly she looked at him almost as
if in fear.
'Perhaps I'm selfish. If you want her, take her, my boy.'

(*Sons and Lovers*)

This extraordinarily intense passage brings to a head many of the emotional complexities of their relationship. The intimate moment is, typically, violently interrupted by the entrance of the father. A quarrel arises between father and son. For the first time Paul threatens to hit him. He defends his mother as a lover would, just as in the Lincoln episode Paul has treated her as if she were his girlfriend.

The crux finally comes when Paul realizes and declares that he cannot love another woman until his mother is dead. We see from Lawrence's statements about the plot that it is at this time that Mrs Morel sees the depth of her hold over her son and chooses to die knowing that this will release him from his agonizing and impossible situation.

After her death, Paul has a final scene with Miriam in which he rejects the possibility of marriage. Their relationship is beyond them both now. He is left with nowhere to go, without mother or mate. He cries out in anguish and despair to his mother, 'She was the only thing that held him up, himself, amid all this. And she was gone . . . ' Here he has another choice to make, that of suicide, of somehow giving up without her. But, as with the choice to marry Miriam, he rejects this choice. The book ends with Lawrence's hero drifting back into life (symbolized by the lights of the town and signalled by the adverb 'quickly') though still rudderless, without direction.

> But no, he would not give in. Turning sharply, he walked towards the city's gold phosphorescence. His fists were shut, his mouth set fast. He would not take that direction, to the darkness, to follow her. He walked towards the faintly humming, glowing town, quickly.

Much of Lawrence's fiction ends with the departure of the central character (in the later books, usually with the woman he loves), escaping from an intolerable situation and heading for a new country, a new civilization. Here this development is not stated, but the implication is that Paul will find a new life beyond the confines of old ties. In the midst of all the choices and rejections he has to make, a small flame of new life is rekindled in the final paragraph.

Opposite Clara Dawes, the suffragette, and wife of Baxter Dawes from whom she is estranged. Paul Morel becomes her lover for a while though he ridicules her women's liberation stance, calling her 'Penelope', a woman really waiting for her man to return to her. Paul is instrument in Clara and Baxter getting back together.

4 *The Rainbow* and *Women in Love*

In 1913 Lawrence began work on a novel that he felt should earn him money. He wanted a pot-boiler, something 'meant . . . for the jeunes filles.' He came to realize as the novel progressed that he was moving away from his first intentions. The subject that were closest to his heart (the relationships between men and women, people and the natural world and society and encroaching industrialization) most occupied him. These could not be contained in an ordinary novel, at least not given expression in the way that he wanted to. He notes ironically halfway through writing this novel that 'it has fallen from grace'. It would not live up to the low standards he had set for it. Indeed, the new novel that he had begun after finishing *Son and Lovers* had grown to such proportions that by 1915 he decided to make two volumes out of it. He initially called it 'The Sisters' (after the two principal female characters, Ursula and Gudrun). It was then changed to 'The Wedding Ring'; and finally, upon dividing it in two, to *The Rainbow* and *Women in Love*.

When Lawrence wrote these novels he was in his creative prime. The latter has become a classic of Modernist fiction, very far from the notions of a populist money-spinning tale. It is another landmark in the

English novel, signalling a major break with the nineteenth-century realism of the social novel. In it, he rejects, to use Lawrence's own terms, 'the old stable ego of character' and 'the certain moral scheme' to explore the ebb and flow of the inner feelings, attempting to get beyond the 'pure object and story'. We saw how *Sons and Lovers* had used both the realist, objective approach and this psychological technique, which was to be seen as peculiarly Modernist. *The Rainbow* continues this fusion, but with *Women in Love*, the split with the past outmoded manner of writing is far more obvious.

Thomas Mann (1875-1955), the German novelist. He is best known for Death in Venice *(1912),* The Magic Mountain *(1924) and* Dr Faustus *(1947). He was a near contemporary of Lawrence who also chose to explore new areas of human existence.*

The Rainbow was published in September 1915, and was within a couple of months suppressed under the Obscene Publications Act. The edition was entirely destroyed. It had offended good taste and received largely hostile reviews from the critics. A revised edition was published in 1926, but the original text did not see the light of day again until 1949. *Women in Love* was published privately in New York in 1920 and in London a year later. Both books, but especially *Women in Love*, which is in many ways significantly different from its predecessor, being more experimental and uncompromising, were misunderstood by most of the literary people of the day. After all, Lawrence's immediate seniors who were writing actively at this time were men like Arnold Bennett, John Galsworthy and H.G. Wells, none of whom seriously questioned the tradition of writing about people and places from an objective point of view, inherited from the nineteeth century. Arnold Bennett was to attack Lawrence for his experimental form in these novels. Lawrence replied to his literary agent. 'Tell Arnold Bennett that all rules of construction hold good only for novels which are copies of other novels. A book which is not a copy of other books has its own construction.' The Modernist movement (in whose camp Lawrence sits rather uneasily, because of his great independence of mind) was finding its expression in the younger writers at about this time but had not yet taken great hold in the minds of the critics. The younger writers, including Lawrence, were men like James Joyce (1882–1941), whose *Ulysses* (another landmark in English fiction) was published in Paris in 1922: Thomas Mann (1875–1955); Marcel Proust (1871–1922); and André Gide (1869–1951). They all experimented with fictional form and with the ways in which fiction conveys reality (or fails to do so). And they were all interested in the inner psychological life of their characters and not simply the external events that shape their lives. Although writing independently of them, Lawrence shares similar interests and anxieties.

The Rainbow

'It is *very* different from *Sons and Lovers*: written in another language almost', Lawrence wrote to his editor and friend, Edward Garnett in 1913. This is true, but perhaps less so of the first part of 'The Sisters' than of the second half, that which was to become the material used in *Women in Love*. *The Rainbow* shares much in common with the great novels of the previous century, such as George Eliot's *Mill on the Floss* and *Middlemarch*; Thomas Hardy's *Far From The Madding Crowd*; and Emily Brontë's *Wuthering Heights*.

It is a novel firmly rooted in the English landscape. It is Lawrence's only major novel that gives a sense of the history of the people that inhabit that landscape, by using several generations of a family to chronicle the changes and events, major and minor, as they happen. The landscape is that which Lawrence knew so intimately, Nottinghamshire and Derbyshire. The family at the centre of the book are the Brangwens, a family of Midlands farmers, Yeomen, independent and proud.

The book covers a period in English history from the 1840s up to the time at which the author was writing. Within this panoramic sweep, Lawrence looks at the lives and loves of three generations of the Brangwen

The Rainbow charts the history of a yeoman family, the Brangwens, from the 1840s into the twentieth century. The early generations farm the land and are shown to be in tune with the slow, forceful rhythms of agricultural England.

family. The historical themes work on two levels: on the one hand there are the people and their inner lives, their private histories; and then there is the backdrop of the greater world outside and beyond them which affects their everyday existence: the growth of industrialization, the spread of the coal mines, the subtly shifting morality of each succeeding generation, representative of the community at large. Lawrence grew up in 'this queer jumble of the old England and the new.' He was acutely aware of the changes going on around him. Many of his feelings about the future of English society are recorded here.

The opening of the book is a powerful evocation of the 'old agricultural England,' which still thrived in the 1840s. The Brangwens of this generation are shown to be in harmony with the natural rhythms of the seasons. They are separated from, and disdainful of, the growing working-class mining communites they see around them. They do not yet see them as a threat to their own way of life:

> They felt the rush of the sap in spring, they knew the wave which cannot halt, but every year throws forward the seed to begetting, and, falling back, leaves the young-born on the earth. They knew the intercourse between heaven and earth, sunshine drawn into the breast and bowels, the rain sucked up in the daytime, nakedness that comes under the wind in Autumn, showing the birds' nests no longer worth hiding. Their lives and interrelations were such; feeling the pulse and body of the soil, that opened to their furrow for the grain . . .

(*The Rainbow*, pp 7–8)

Opposite Markets were an integral part of the life of the rural community. Tom Brangwen takes Anna once a week to the market near Marsh Farm. There she sees with foreign eyes the life and vitality of the people going about their business of buying and selling.

The language of the passage above is of particular interest. It has something about it of the rhythms of the English Authorized Version of the Bible. Lawrence was steeped in the prose of the Bible from an early age. In the context of the novel, this slightly stilted and difficult tone gives the early Brangwens the significance of Biblical figures, and distances them in time from the reader. They are given a semi-mythical status.

The men feel a 'blood intimacy' with the rhythms of natural life. They bend the natural world to their own ends but are in turn receptive to its influences. They are slow, profound people and Lawrence links their life's blood pulsing to the beat of the earth. The relationship between farmer and land is revealed as organic, healthy and based on respect.

In 1913 Lawrence first set down in words his ideas about the importance and significance of the term 'blood consciousness'. He wrote to a friend in that year that,

My great religion is a belief in the blood, the flesh, as being wiser than the intellect. We can go wrong in our minds. But what the blood feels, and believes, says, is always true.

From this idea, Lawrence was to create a vast scheme of beliefs that amounts to a doctrine or philosophy of life. This will be looked at in further detail in Chapter 7. It is enough here to note that the wisdom of the blood, or the instincts, gives Lawrence's characters a harmonious relationship with the natural world. With the onset of industrialization, this was to change radically. One reason for Lawrence's horror of industrial growth and urban living, was that it separated people from the cycles of the natural world. In doing this, it also separated them from themselves and from each other. The mechanized world puts an emphasis on the mental life, on the intellect, at the expense of the feelings and bodily sensations. Lawrence explores the implications of this in both novels. The onset of industrialization is shown in the novel with the opening of a canal in 1840 which crosses Brangwen land. It is the first intrusion from the outside world, and is a symbol of change.

The Rainbow draws on the Bible in other ways. The presentation of history by telling the lives of different generations is a technique used in the Book of Genesis. The Brangwen history begins with Tom and his Polish emigré wife, Lydia Lensky. Their struggle for fulfilment is told, until the next generation takes centre stage and they fade into the background. Will and Anna Brangwen enact their particular relationship and then give way to their children, Gudrun and Ursula. With the last of these we have arrived at a time near Lawrence's own and the writing style changes. Lawrence is less concerned with distancing himself from his characters because now they are familiar to him, creatures of his own time. Ursula and Gudrun are modern women, far more independent than their mother, Anna; or their grandmother, Lydia.

The title of the book suggests that Lawrence was deliberately drawing parallels with the Bible. The Rainbow in the Old Testament is a sign from God, sent after the flood in which all but Noah and his family perished, that God would never again use this form of destruction. The rainbow in the world of nature appears to form a bridge between heaven and earth. Lawrence uses the symbol of the rainbow to suggest a relationship both between men and women, and between people and the natural world. When the rainbow is broken it is an emblem of a lack of fulfilment in a relationship. For

Opposite As the historical sweep of The Rainbow *progresses, the influence of industrialization is increasingly felt. Ursula's final vision sets the deadening and dehumanizing effects of mechanization against the new hope of a different set of relationships symbolized by the rainbow itself over-arching the earth.*

Rainbow

instance, Tom Brangwen, when feeling excluded from his pregnant wife Lydia, retreats into himself, and is described as being ' . . . like a broken arch thrust sickeningly out from support.' On a far greater scale, the rainbow appears at the end of the book as a symbol of hope, just as in the Bible it is used to signify a new, stronger relationship between God and man. Ursula, after having been through several stages of personal development and a disastrous relationship, climbs out of despair through a vision of a new world to come in which people attain a far greater understanding of each other and achieve self-fulfilment.

> She saw the stiffened bodies of the colliers, which seemed already enclosed in a coffin, she saw their unchanging eyes, the eyes of those buried alive: she saw the hard, cutting edges of the new houses, which seemed to spread over the hillside in their insentient triumph, a triumph of horrible, amorphous angles and straight lines . . . and she was sick with a nausea so deep that she perished as she sat.
>
> (*The Rainbow*, p.495)

Against this dreadful vision of industrialization Lawrence sets this vision of the rainbow:

> And then, in the blowing clouds, she saw a band of faint iridescence colouring in faint colours a portion of the hill . . . Steadily the colour gathered, mysteriously, from nowhere, it took presence upon itself, there was a faint, vast rainbow. The arc bended and strengthened itself till it arched indomitable, making great architecture of light and colour and the space of heaven, its pedestals luminous in the corruption of new houses on the low hill, its arch the top of heaven.
>
> (*The Rainbow*, p. 495)

Opposite The sketch Lawrence made upon completing The Rainbow *in early 1915. From this we can see the importance for the author of the contrast between the man-made ugly environment and the beauty and simplicity of the natural architecture of the rainbow.*

Below The sight of the 'stiffened bodies of the colliers' nauseates Ursula. On one level The Rainbow *is a powerful attack upon those who exploit men and women merely to make money, whilst perpetuating their lives of drudgery.*

Human architecture of house and factory are set against the natural architecture of the rainbow: the first seen as corrupt and the other cleansing and new. In the final revelation, Ursula sees the 'old, brittle corruption . . . swept away, the world built up in a living fabric of Truth, fitting to the over-arching heaven.'

Ursula is the most articulate person in the novel. She is a schoolteacher and has herself received a good education. Lawrence gives her the greatest potential for self-fulfilment. Each generation of lovers and parents are measured against their potential for fulfilment. Lawrence shows us that each generation has a wider horizon, a greater scope and potential than those before it. The lives of Tom and Lydia find limited expression in their marriage. During Will and Anna's wedding, in the middle of a drunken speech, Tom proclaims that 'a

Not far from the pits with their mountains of ash and back-to-back miners' cottages were the fields and farms of an older, more durable England.

married couple makes an Angel'. Tom is shown to achieve a measure of contentment in his marriage to Lydia. But he is killed in a flood, which on the mythical level relates to the flood of the Bible, the ultimate symbol of failure, just as the rainbow is seen as the supreme symbol of success.

Anna, his stepdaughter (she is Lydia's daughter by a previous husband) is shown as an obstinate, strong-willed woman. But her life becomes enclosed by her husband and the children she bears. It is left to Ursula to attempt to find fulfilment.

Where *Women in Love* picks up the story Ursula and her sister, Gudrun, both unmarried, hover on the edge of wider experiences in the world at large. *Women in Love* carries on from a very different perspective and with very different aims.

Women in Love

The Rainbow is basically optimistic in outlook. Lawrence felt that society could turn aside from its course of self-destruction and that individuals could find ultimate freedom of self-expression and fulfilment, in themselves and through their lovers. One critic and friend said of this book that it had:

> . . . a serenity and leisureliness which are absent from his first three novels and did not survive the First World War and the persecution inflicted on him for writing this literary masterpiece.

The war had begun in 1914. By the time Lawrence came to write his new novel, the war had spilt enough blood to sicken him to the heart and make him despair completely of there ever being a revival in human values. Lawrence was well aware of the changes in himself and in his writing. In a letter to a friend written in July 1917, he was to comment:

> About *The Rainbow*: it was all written before the war, though revised during September and October of 1914. I don't think the war had much to do with it – I don't think the war altered it, from its pre-war statement . . . I knew, as I revised the book, that it was a kind of working up to the dark sensual or Dionysic or Aphrodisiac ecstacy, which does actually burst the world-consciousness in every individual. There is another novel, sequel to *The Rainbow*, called *Women in Love* . . . This actually does contain the results in one's soul of the war: it is purely destructive . . .

Only a few years before he had been writing to friends that he felt 'hopeful . . . I know we shall all come through, rise again and walk healed and whole and new, in a big inheritance, here on earth.' But 1915 was a personally disappointing year, the year in which *The Rainbow* was published and then confiscated by the authorities. Late that year he was to say in a letter,

> I think there is no future for England: only a decline and fall. That is the dreadful and unbearable part of it: to have been born into a decadent era, a decline of life, a collapsing civilization.

He had been confident that *The Rainbow* could show that relationships between people had gone wrong, and point in the direction of new and better ways. The cure, as he saw it, was 'a readjustment between men and women, and a making free and healthy of the sex.' It is ironical that his novel should have been reviewed as something unwholesome. One reviewer wrote:

A thing like *The Rainbow* has no right to exist in the wind of war. It is a greater menace to our public health than any of the epidemic diseases which we pay our medical officers to fight . . . The young men who are dying for liberty are moral beings . . . The life they lay down is a lofty thing. Not the thing that creeps and crawls in this novel.

Lawrence, Katherine Mansfield, Frieda and Middleton Murry on the day of the Lawrences' wedding, in 1914. Lawence was at the height of his creative power and his outlook on life was generally very bouyant and hopeful. This optimism lies at the heart of The Rainbow *and is noticeably absent in* Women in Love.

Women in Love continues the story of the sisters, Ursula and Gudrun. Ursula's search for a fulfilling life, started in *The Rainbow*, is continued, and is one of the major themes of the novel. The novel takes us from the provincial world of the Brangwens and Marsh Farm, to the metropolitan world of London, and the Bohemian set of artists and writers who gather there. Lawrence uses the technique of mixing scenes of descriptive realism with moments of ritualistic or mystic significance. *The Rainbow* had done this successfully (in scenes such as the sheaf-gathering episode in Chapter 4, in which Anna and Will draw together in circumstances of highly-charged though restrained emotional intensity, or in Chapter 15, where Ursula and Anton walk and talk under the moonlight. The language the characters use is deliberately ordinary and powerless in the face of the great passion that wells up between them). The earlier book skilfully combines two different styles to convey both the external events of life and the internal rhythms of individual characters. *Women in Love* further develops language and style to express the non-human or super-human passions that shake the characters out of their social selves and reduce them to their essential selves, their true natures. At the time of writing, Lawrence was writing a study of Thomas Hardy, a writer he greatly admired. In striving to understand Hardy, Lawrence wrote about his own technique. He himself could be included in the list of great writers who have the gift of seeing the changeless nature of human beings beyond the changing circumstances of day to day life:

> . . . the quality Hardy shares with the great writers, Shakespeare or Sophocles or Tolstoi, this setting behind the small action of his protagonists the terrific action of unfathomed nature, setting a smaller system of morality, the one grasped and formulated by the human consciousness within the vast, uncomprehended and incomprehensible morality of nature or of life itself, surpassing human consciousness.

Lawrence believes that individual sanity is achieved only by keeping in contact with the larger morality of life itself. The main channel of contact is through the 'blood' – blood consciousness rather than the purely mental life he associates with modern existence. At the

heart of the matter are sexual relations, where individual
consciousness can be lost in the larger life of the unconscious. For Lawrence, correct sexual relations (which
have nothing to do with the simple facts of marriage or
procreation) are the single most recuperative and neces-
sary relations.

Gerald Crich, son of the local colliery owner, exerts his willpower over the horse he rides by forcing it, against its nature, to race alongside the fast and noisy train. The scene shows Gerald's belief in strength and domination as a means to achieving desired goals.

Ursula and Gudrun are two contrasted individuals. When the novel opens, Gudrun has lately returned from London to her home town in the Midlands.

> Gudrun, new from her life in Chelsea and Sussex, shrank cruelly from this amorphous ugliness of a small colliery town in the Midlands . . . she felt like a beetle toiling in the dust.

The novel revolves around the sisters' relationships with two men, Rupert Birkin, a government schools inspector and Gerald Crich, the son of the largest colliery owner in the area. These are two very different men. Gerald is masterful, physically well-developed and a sportsman. Rupert is frail and pale and something of an intellectual and cynic. He voices many of the author's own bitter and cynical responses to modern life. He is totally disillusioned, with himself as well as with life around him. Birkin is trapped in a destructive relationship with Hermione Roddice, a wealthy patron. She, along with Gerald and ultimately Gudrun, are revealed as being types of the mental world, unresponsive to tenderness and the emotions. One of the central contradictions of the novel, which give it its power, is the sense that individuals seek salvation through relationships with other people, but that in general their relationships are unsuccessful. Birkin is acutely discontented and unconsciously searches for the ideal partner with whom he can find fulfilment. He finds this in Ursula, whose openness and responsiveness attract him.

However, before he can marry her, he has to educate her in what he sees as being love's true shape. He is the self-styled priest of love, a prophet, who starts with complicated ideas which are modified by his experiences. He believes passionately in a world and force beyond the human will. He detests the mechanized life of the men whom Gerald employs down the mines and he hates the artificial social structure of England. He is the most socially mobile character in the book because he refuses to play his part in the class structure. The book ends with his flight abroad with Ursula to alien cultures to escape the deadening weight of England, where he feels he has to be what he is not.

The dirty and noisy workings of a colliery. It is against such a background as this that Gerald bends the will of his workers and forms his theories about human nature.

The love he believes in is one in which individuals remain true to themselves but find a greater life in union with another person.

> On the whole, he hated sex, it was such a limitation. It was sex that turned men into a broken half of a couple, the woman into the other broken half. And he wanted to be single in himself, the woman single in herself. He wanted sex to revert to the level of the other appetites, to be regarded as a functional process, not as a fulfilment. He believed in sex marriage. But beyond this, he wanted a further conjunction, where man had being and woman had being, two pure beings each constituting the freedom of the other, balancing each other like two poles of one force, like two angels, or two demons.

The relationship between Gerald and Rupert is another form of love. Rupert explains to Gudrun that he needs the love of Gerald, though they are such different men. Rupert despises Gerald's materialism, while Gerald distrusts the other's unworldliness.

> Gerald really loved Birkin, though he never quite believed in him. Birkin was too unreal; – clever, whimsical, wonderful, but not practical enough. Gerald felt that his own understanding was much sounder and safe. Birkin was delightful, a wonderful spirit, but after all, not to be taken seriously, not quite to be counted as a man amongst men.

Gerald perishes, frozen to death in the Alps while on holiday with the sisters and Birkin. Lawrence shows that for all his understanding of the practical world of men, he is a child when it comes to the emotional world. His relationship with Gudrun goes wrong and the tensions between them bring about his death. He dies in the environment of cold snow and ice, symbols of the inhuman world where all warmth and tenderness are absent. *Women in Love* is an apocalyptic novel. It refers continually to hell and damnation in relation to the way in which modern people live and conduct their relationships. Gerald's death is a symbol, as well as a tragedy on a human scale, of the vision Lawrence has for the fate of the world, led as it is by men like Gerald. But Lawrence had his hero turn aside from any attempt to

preach to society on how to heal itself. Instead, he settles for individual love and fulfilment. Ursula is for him 'sheer intimacy' and an eternal companion.

Woman in Love is one of Lawrence's major achievements. It is his longest novel and one of the most discussed. In it he broke new ground by portraying the inner lives and motives of his characters. He reached great depths of bitterness and despair, but found some measure of consolation for Ursula and Birkin in each other, and in their rejections of the values of a civilization in decline. Lawrence could no longer be positive about society at large healing itself – personal suffering at the hands of the authorities and the monstrous calamity of the First World War had put paid to that. He was to leave England almost for good after the war, to travel the world in his own personal quest for fulfilment.

Gerald Crich perishes alone in a white world of cold and snow, both symbols for Lawrence of the inhuman. On one level, it is an inevitable end for this character.

5 Lawrence's Shorter Fiction

Opposite A scene from the film of The Virgin and the Gypsy: *the middle-class, repressed daughter of the vicar comes under the spell of the elemental gypsy, and moves unsteadily into a more passionate existence.*

Throughout his life, Lawrence wrote many short stories. His first short story was a piece called 'A Prelude', which appeared in the *Nottinghamshire Guardian* in 1907, under the name of Jessie Chambers, and he continued to write them well beyond the completion of *Lady Chatterley's Lover* (1928), his last major novel. They vary considerably in length, tone and scope. Pieces like 'Smile' and 'Things' are really little more than sketches. Whereas 'St. Mawr', 'The Captain's Doll' and 'The Virgin and the Gipsy' almost amount to small novels, though they do not have the breadth and detail of background material that we expect in a fully-fledged novel.

Lawrence went through several definite periods of development as a creative writer. His settings and subject matter changed as he travelled to different countries and absorbed new experiences. It changed from the intimate presentation of his beloved Midlands, to Europe (especially Germany and Italy, where he spent considerable time) and on to Australia, Sri Lanka, Mexico and New Mexico (in the USA). He wrote constantly about the places he visited and the people he met in them.

Not only do the settings for his novels and short stories change to reflect these new places, but so also does his subject matter. Often his attitude to things changes rather than the things themselves. The short stories reflect his changing moods and opinions as much as the longer works. Indeed, many of them deal with circumstances and stories that appear in the novels, though in

slightly altered form. 'The Virgin and The Gipsy' (first
published in 1925) has for its theme the power of a
'natural' man (the gipsy) over the emotions and feelings
of an educated middle-class young woman, the daughter
of a vicar. She feels stifled by her environment, by the
passionless and sterile world in which she lives, and
her young heart yearns for something beyond these con-
straints. The liberation comes through contact with the

The Lawrences in Teotihuacan in Mexico in 1924 with some local Indians. Lawrence's contact with the life here and in New Mexico gave rise to the stories 'The Woman Who Rode Away' and The Plumed Serpent.

gipsy, a man who stands for the power of instinct, the blood-feeling. This theme is reworked by Lawrence in *Lady Chatterley's Lover*, though the actual circumstances and setting of the novel bear no resemblance to those of the short story.

Lawrence was an exploratory artist, never content to remain on the same ground. He said, 'The business of art is to reveal the relation between man and his circumambient universe, at the living moment. As mankind is always struggling in the foils of old relationships, art is always ahead of the times.' He made his greatest leaps into new areas of psychological realism in the major novels and pushed his prose into the realism of myth-making and symbolism. In attempting new methods in fiction he was not always entirely successful. *Women in Love*, for instance, is often criticized for being too dogmatic. In the short stories, Lawrence was more content to concentrate on the tale itself, rather than to urge a morality or explain his beliefs. For this reason, many critics believe that the short stories are more successful than the novels. They are clearer in terms of construction and effect. Lawrence the author keeps himself distanced from his material and so is better able to be objective about it. He intrudes less with his own presence or with a character used as a mouthpiece to spout forth his undigested philosophy. 'The Woman Who Rode Away,' (written in 1924) for example, is generally agreed to be a better piece of fiction than *The Plumed Serpent*, a novel dealing with a similar subject matter: the meeting of Western consciousness and values, embodied in a white woman, with the primitive, ritualistic consciousness of ancient Mexican Indians. In both, death (whether symbolic or actual) at the hands of the elemental powers of an older civilization, represent the extinction of Western consciousness, which she represents: of hollow materialism and hollow Christianity. Lawrence himself experienced something of a ritual death and resurrection in his exposure to the ancient in Mexico and New Mexico:

> I think New Mexico was the greatest experience from the outside world that I have ever had. It certainly changed me for ever. Curious as it may sound, it was New Mexico that liberated me from the present era of civilization, the great era of material and mechanical development.

'The Woman Who Rode Away' is more successful in presenting its theme because it allows the action to reveal the message. In *The Plumed Serpent*, Lawrence intrudes to preach. His theme is less unified and the power of the tale is diluted, to some extent.

The collections of short stories bear a loose relationship with the major novels on which Lawrence was working at the time. These main collections are: *A Modern Lover* (the stories here relate to his early period in the Midlands, and use techniques of realism, such as objective detail and dialogue, written at the time of his first novel, *The White Peacock*); *The Prussian Officer* (from the period of *Sons and Lovers* and his meeting Frieda); *England, My*

Lawrence had been published in The English Review *since 1909, when some of his poems were included by the editor, Ford Madox Ford. This is the first page of his short story, 'England, My England,' which appeared in 1915.*

England, My England

By D. H. Lawrence

I.

THE dream was still stronger than the reality. In the dream he was at home on a hot summer afternoon, working across the little stream at the bottom of the garden, carrying the garden path in continuation on to the common. He had cut the rough turf and the bracken, and left the grey, dryish soil bare. He was troubled because he could not get the path straight. He had set up his sticks, and taken the sights between the big pine-trees, but for some unknown reason everything was wrong. He looked again through the strong, shadowy pine-trees as through a doorway, at the green garden-path rising between sunlit flowers, tall purple and white columbines. Always, tense with anxiety, he saw the rising flowery garden and the sloping old roof of the cottage, beyond the intervening shadow, as in a mirage.

There was the sound of children's voices calling and talking: high, childish, girlish voices, plaintive, slightly didactic, and tinged with hard authoritativeness. "If you don't come soon, Nurse, I shall run out there where there are snakes."

Always this conflict of authority, echoed even in the children! His heart was hard with disillusion. He worked on in the gnawing irritation and resistance.

Set in resistance, he was all the time clinched upon himself. The sunlight blazed down upon the earth; there was a vividness of flamy vegetation and flowers, of tense seclusion amid the peace of the commons. The cottage with its great sloping roofs slept in the for-ever sunny hollow, hidden, eternal. And here he lived, in this ancient, changeless hollow of flowers and sunshine and the sloping-roofed house. It was balanced like a nest in a bank, this hollow home, always full of peace, always under heaven

England (written during the First World War, and relating to the period of *The Rainbow* and *Women in Love*); a series of longer stories, 'The Ladybird', 'The Fox', and 'The Captain's Doll' (composed after the war – the last of these is set in post-war Austria); 'St. Mawr', 'The Princess' and 'The Woman Who Rode Away' (all written in the early 1920s, taking Mexico and New Mexico as their themes); and finally, late stories, including 'The Virgin and the Gipsy' and 'The Escaped Cock' (a retelling of the Christ story, in which Christ rises from the dead and instead of carrying on with his mission as saviour of mankind, decides instead to live his own life, to affirm life in the flesh rather than life in the spirit. This is one of Lawrence's most powerful pieces of fable-writing, in which he puts all his belief in the life on earth as a positive good, written at a time when he knew he was dying from tuberculosis).

Lawrence maintained a keen interest in painting until many of his works were seized at an exhibition in London in 1929. He was a gifted landscape painter, though it was for his human figures that he fell foul of the censors.

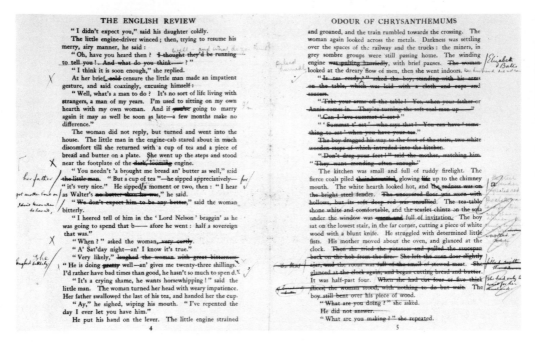

Lawrence wrote 'Odour of Chrysanthemums' in 1909 and it later appeared in The English Review. *These are proofs corrected by Lawrence.*

'Odour of Chrysanthemums' demonstrates well Lawrence's craftmanship in the short story. It is an early story, which first appeared in print in the *English Review* in 1911, and in the collection *The Prussian Officer* in 1914. It is set in a Midlands mining town and centres on a woman waiting for her husband to return from the pits. Lawrence skilfully builds up the tension as time passes and he still has not arrived. We discover there has been a fall at the coal-face where he was working late, and he has been killed. He is brought home by his workmates, and wife and mother wash his body and prepare him for burial. These are the bones of the story. The technique Lawrence uses has been called 'poetic realism'. He invests this domestic tragedy with tremendous power and dignity, lifting it out of the ordinary, to suggest things about the lives of the couple and to contrast the reactions of the two women to the news and their reception of his body.

We gradually realize that husband and wife scarcely knew each other in life. The irony is that it takes his death for her to discover this shattering truth.

> There had been nothing between them, and yet they had come together, exchanging their nakedness

repeatedly. Each time he had taken her, they had been two isolated beings, far apart as now . . . For as she looked at the dead man, her mind, cold and detached, said clearly: 'Who am I? What have I been doing? I have been fighting a husband who did not exist. *He* existed all the time, what wrong have I done? What was that I have been living with? There lies the reality, this man.

His wife, Elizabeth, is a typical Laurentian character: domineering and constantly looking to better herself in the eyes of society. But both husband and wife are transformed by the tragedy. The realistic prose of the opening gives way to ritualistic, poetic prose when she reflects on what their life together has really meant. The symbol of the chrysanthemums gains meaning as the story gathers its force: chysanthemums are present at each rite of passage — at their marriage, at the birth of their child, and they are in the room in which his body is laid. They become linked with him and with his death.

The story offers very little comfort. These are the facts of life. But in Elizabeth, in spite of her realization of her isolation and future loneliness, Lawrence invests stoical strength. She is alive, and she must continue in her life, such as it is. The mystery of death is for the dead and that of life is for the living. 'She knew she submitted to life, which was her immediate master. But from death, her ultimate master, she winced with fear and shame.'

Manuscript additions made by Lawrence to the first proofs of 'Odour of Chrysanthemums'. This powerful short story combines realism with an early experiment into the more difficult realms of human feelings and inarticulated thought.

85

6 Lawrence's Poetry

In the same way as the novels and short stories, Lawrence's poetry has strong links with the phases of his life. In the Preface to his *Last Poems*, a friend and fellow-poet, Richard Aldington, wrote:

> Lawrence's writing was not something outside himself, it was part of himself, it came out of his life and in turn fed his life. He adventured into himself in order to write, and by writing discovered himself.

Lawrence regarded his poetry as fragmented autobiography. He started to write poems late in his teens and he continued to do so right up until he death in 1930. The very earliest poems are, compared with what he was to achieve, derivative, drawing on Hardy and Meredith and the Pre-Raphaelites. These include such poems as 'To Guelder Roses' and 'To Campions'. Lawrence in his early experiments also stuck to traditional forms of lyric poetry, using rhyme and metre. But he was soon to develop his own voice and strike out on his own with a form more suited to his content. He wrote in 1913 to a friend:

Opposite A manuscript page of Lawrence's poem, 'Discipline'. He wrote poetry throughout his short but intense writing career, collecting them in thirteen volumes, including Look! We Have Come Through!, Pansies *and* Last Poems.

> I think I read my poetry more by length than by stress – as a matter of movements in space than footsteps hitting the earth . . . It all depends on the *pause* – the natural pause, the natural *lingering* of the voice according to the feeling – it is the hidden *emotional* pattern that makes poetry, not the obvious form . . .

Discipline

'Tis stormy, and raindrops cling like silver
    bees to the panes
The thin sycamore in the garden is swinging
    with flattened leaves
The heads of my boys move dimly through
    the yellow gloom that stains
The class : over them all the darkness of my
    discipline weaves.

It is no good, my dear, gentleness ~~&~~ forbearance
    – I endured too long.
I have pushed my hands ~~into~~ the dark soil
    under the flowers of my soul
Under the caress of leaves, and felt where the
    roots were strong
Fixed and grappling in the darkness for the
    deep-soil's little control

'Tis no good, my darling, life does not lead us
    with a daisy chain
We are schooled by pain, and only in suffering
    are we brothers
So I've torn some roots from my soul, & twisted them
    good or bane
Into thongs of discipline : from my anguished submission
    weaving another's.

He dropped rhyming poetry for free verse, because he considered form to come naturally from the strength of feeling contained in the poem. He needed the freedom from purely mechanical impositions, such as rhyme and metre, to write truly about his experiences and the way in which he held them. His free verse is shown in the poem 'Little Fish':

The tiny fish enjoy themselves in the sea.
Quick little splinters of life, their little lives are fun to
    them in the sea.

In Lawrence's lifetime he published ten volumes of poetry. It took far longer for the general public to regard him as a poet than it did for them to see him as a novelist. Even today, his reputation as a poet is not great, and certainly not as great as it should be.

In 1920 the Lawrences were in Sicily at a place called Taormina. Here he wrote such poems as 'Bare Fig-Trees', 'Bare Almond-Trees' and 'Hibiscus and Salvia Flowers'. Indeed many of his poems are suffused with the landscape, the flora and the fauna of mediterranean lands.

The periods in which he wrote his poetry fall into distinct groupings. His early poems were written about his life in Eastwood and Nottingham, and, as one would expect, contain a great deal to do with his mother and with Jessie Chambers. Another group of poems, called collectively *Look! We Have Come Through*, cover his early life with Frieda, their travels in Italy and Germany and their struggles with each other's personality. *Birds, Beasts and Flowers* were written later, with influence drawn from the Italian countryside and Mexico. *Pansies* is a difficult collection which Lawrence called 'a handful of

Piazza del Duomo e Fontana, Taormina.

thoughts'. (The title is a play on the french word, *pensées*, meaning 'thoughts'). They are bitter pieces written against the ills of society, 'my tender administrations to the mental and emotional wounds we suffer'. He goes on to say in his introduction to the collection: 'Each little piece is a thought . . . which comes as much from from the heart and genitals as from the head.' However, many of them are little more than ill-tempered railings and not really the stuff of great poetry. Many object to the values and manifestations of modern society. There are the hatreds that we have seen in his novels, as in the poem, 'Let Us Be Men':

> For God's sake, let us be men
> not monkeys minding machines
> or sitting with our tails curled
> while the machine amuses us, the radio or film or
> gramophone.
>
> Monkeys with a bland grin on our faces. –

Last Poems is a collection written with the knowledge of death in mind. Some of his greatest and most well-known poems, such as 'The Ship of Death' are in this collection. This poem is a meditation on his own death, written with great dignity and power. It is full of images of decline and decomposition, set against fertile nature and the life-giving forces:

> Now it is Autumn and the falling fruit
> and the long journey towards oblivion.
>
> The apples falling like great drops of dew
> to bruise themselves an exit from themselves.

In this first stanza Lawrence puts death in the context of the great scheme of things. In nature (represented by the apples falling, the fruit and then the bruise) as in human life, death is inevitable. 'The grim frost is at hand', he says. But the poem can be seen as optimistic:

> Build then the ship of death, for you must take the
> longest journey, to oblivion.
>
> And die the death, the long and painful death that lies
> between the old self and the new.

Lawrence attempts to pierce the mystery of death, and his own feelings about the survival of the soul in the frail ship sailing on to a new dawn. The poem is written from a point outside himself. He uses the second person, 'you', throughout the poem, and the object is ambiguous: he is at once addressing an audience ('Oh build your ship of death') and himself, as if he stands beyond himself looking down. He was working on this poem when he died.

Each collection of Lawrence's poetry is best read in full. Each poem adds to the experience of the previous

one. Lawrence rarely if ever revised his poems: they come directly from experience, and their success or failure is due to their spontaneity. 'I want to write live things, if crude and half formed.' This is their secret. They are not intellectually crafted in the manner of the poetry of W.B. Yeats or T.S. Eliot. They are on occasions closer to trance-induced outpourings. They are in turn deceptively simple and strikingly original. Like the great early Romantic poet, William Blake, Lawrence's poetry is elemental and often stark. But it offers great rewards to the persistent reader.

The house on Kiowa Ranch. The buffalo on the wall was painted by Taos Indians on hearing of Lawrence's death.

7 Lawrence's Philosophy

Lawrence, in the major novels from *The Rainbow* onwards, increasingly saw fiction as a vehicle for ideas, and was less content to let the fiction speak for itself. His shorter stories remain simple in technique: indeed they often convey a lesson through the mode of fable. But *The Rainbow, Women in Love* and *The Plumed Serpent* contain large sections in which Lawrence preaches a philosophy which is anti-materialistic, and against modern life-styles that he saw as too self-conscious and lacking in tenderness and feeling. He saw modern society as being chronically sick. The horror and madness of the First World War reinforced this feeling in him. He did not profess to be a philosopher, but he struggled to form conclusions from the raw materials of life. He expressed them in his writings in order to show how society could be retrieved from the chaos towards which he saw twentieth-century life moving.

In 1913 Lawrence first spoke of his 'belief': 'My great religion is a belief in the blood.' He was to repeat this belief in various forms in fiction, travel essays, poems and philosophical treatises for the rest of his life. Lawrence himself was aware of the dangers of trying to reduce a novel, which is about the complex processes of human existence and relations, to a dogmatic set of ideas, independent of actual lived and felt experience. He was aware of this tendency in himself, and warns us: 'Never trust the artist, trust the tale'. He had no doubt that the novel presents a world closer to human truths than that inhabited by the philosophers, men like Bertrand Russell. He was also acutely aware that the

Opposite The horror of the First World War reinforced Lawrence's belief that modern society was hopelessly sick.

92

'novel's spirit is the spirit of complexity'. The novel does not provide simple answers to grand questions about our existence. But part of Lawrence's character drove him to try to establish absolutes, to look for certainty and stability:

> . . . even art is utterly dependent on philosophy: or if you prefer it, on a metaphysic. The metaphysic may not be everywhere very accurately stated, and may be quite unconscious in the artist, yet it is a metaphysic that governs men all the time.
>
> *(Fantasia of the Unconscious)*

At the centre of his philosophy is human life and potential. He saw this life in relation to the larger world of nature, and indeed spoke about the non-human life of birds, beasts and flowers, which both fascinated him and left him in awe of their separateness from human existence. Many of his poems deal with his attempts to come to terms with the lives of things that do not think or feel or react in the same way that people do.

> I don't know fishes . . .

he states bluntly in the poem, 'Fish'.

> No fingers, no hands and feet, no lips;
> No tender muzzles,
> No wistful bellies,
> No loins of desire,
> None.

But the hearts and minds and motives of people he understood to a profound degree. And he understood what he felt was missing from people's lives, in the sterile, twentieth-century world. With the advent of modern science, man, according to Lawrence, had become increasingly separated from real life:

> For man, as for flower, beast and bird, the supreme triumph is to be most vividly, most perfectly alive. Whatever the unborn and the dead may know, they cannot know the beauty, the marvel of being alive in the flesh.
>
> *(Apocalypse, 1931)*

At the heart of Lawrence's beliefs, expressed both in his words and his paintings, was the larger life of the natural world, of bird, beast and flower.

The intellect, and its servant, the machine, had been developed at the expense of intuition, feelings and the inner life. Lawrence portrays in his novels various characters who are only half alive to the wonders of the flesh, the world of the sensations. Gerald Crich in *Women in Love*, for instance, is master of other men, of machines and also dominates horses (see Chapter 9); but he is shown to be at the mercy of the deep forces of his emotions. He is a child in spite of his physical prowess and dominant will. Similarly, Clifford Chatterley and friends like Tommy Dukes, in *Lady Chatterley's Lover*, are revealed as half-formed, inadequate people, in that mentally they can understand life and sex and emotions, but in their actions they evade full experience, even proving to be literally sterile.

For Lawrence, the key lay in an understanding of all human needs. He did not deny the intellect its appetite. He was, after all, a working-class intellectual himself. But he distrusted an intellect cut loose from the rest of

Robin Hood's Well in Abbey Wood, Nottinghamshire thought to be the site drawn upon by Lawrence in describing the hut in Lady Chatterley's Lover.

life. This is where his 'blood religion' or 'blood consciousness' is important. He placed the powers of intuition in 'the blood' and in dwelling upon these unconscious or sub-conscious urges he hoped to find salvation for modern man. The sexual life was only part of the overall route to health and sanity. It has perhaps been dwelt upon by some commentators too much.

Birkin, in *Women in Love*, most nearly approaches Lawrence's ideal. His views on love introduce another aspect of Lawrence's doctrine. He seeks a state beyond romantic love and fidelity. He sees the universe in terms of opposites, these would include light and dark, good and bad, moon and sun, motion and inertia, and of course, male and female. Birkin believes in the separate identities of the male and female, and for him fulfilment lies in the recognition of difference and the striving towards a balanced state of creative tension between the two opposites. This is not an easy concept, but it is fundamental to understanding Lawrence's ideal.

And there is no rest, no cessation from the conflict. For we are two opposites which exist by virtue of our inter-opposition. Remove the opposition and there is collapse, a sudden crumbling into universal darkness.

Most of the non-fiction Lawrence wrote in the form of treatises and essays belongs to the middle period of his career, from around 1914 to about 1922. In this period he wrote his *Study of Thomas Hardy*, which relates more to Lawrence's thought then it does strictly to Hardy. *The Crown* (1915) is another important piece written about his philosophy. *Psychoanalysis and the Unconscious* is a small book in which Lawrence attempts to relate the new teachings of Sigmund Freud to his own system.

Apocalypse was one of the last works on which he worked before his death. It relates chronologically and in sentiment to 'The Man Who Died' and the poem 'The Ship of Death'. In it he asserts, as a dying man, his great belief in the life of the flesh. It is extraordinary to think that as his body deteriorated he could assert more strongly his belief in flesh and blood. It places his philosophy firmly in the natural world. For him, God is made real in the things of beauty seen around him: birds, beast and flowers. In 'The Man Who Died', his last short story written in the form of a philosophical fable, he brings together Christianity, which was a major influence on his life and thought, and his own belief in the here and now. The story shows a Christ figure resurrected after the crucifixion, who chooses life having known death. The Christ figure slowly awakens to the wonder of the world around him after the cold negation of the tomb.

> Slowly, slowly he crept down from the cell of rock with the caution of the bitterly wounded. Bandages and linen and perfume fell away, and he crouched on the ground against the wall of rock, to recover oblivion. But he saw his hurt feet touching the earth again, with unspeakable pain, the earth they had meant to touch no more . . . To be back! To be back again, after all that!

Opposite The Lawrence Memorial Chapel at Kiowa Ranch, New Mexico. Although Lawrence died in Vence, France, his ashes were taken to the chapel in 1935.

Frieda, his wife, said of Lawrence after his death that the immeasurable gift he had given to his fellow man was 'the splendour of living, the hope of more and more life'. This is at the centre of his thoughts and beliefs.

Glossary

Bloomsbury set The name given to a group of literary and artistic friends who met regularly from about 1906 onwards. They included Virginia and Leonard Woolf, Vanessa and Clive Bell, David Garnett, Duncan Grant, E. M. Forster, Lytton Strachey and Roger Fry.

Characterization The technique used by an author to portray significant aspects of people in a novel.

Cynic A person who believes that human conduct is based upon self-interest, and who consequently takes refuge behind a satirical or sneering attitude.

Dialect Variation in a language in terms of accent or vocabulary, often associated with a region or social group.

Free verse (*vers libre*) Distinguished from traditional verse by its lack of set rhyming patterns and irregular metrics.It relies on the larger movement of the stanza rather than that of the line.

Industrialization Relating to the large-scale manufacture of goods and the spreading factory system that embodied the processes by which this was achieved.

Materialism An attitude to life in which the means to physical and social well-being are stressed at the expense of other aspects of existence (for example, the aesthetic, the artistic or the spiritual).

Metaphysics The science that investigates the beginnings of existence and knowledge.

Metrics Relating to the structure of poetry, in terms of the syllables (both stressed and unstressed) in a line.

Modernism A movement started early this century which aimed to describe human psychological reality and the inner, emotional life, as opposed to delineating the day-to-day outer forms of existence, prevalent in nineteenth-century writings.

Philosophy A word that means 'love of wisdom'. Once it described all investigations into the workings of the natural world, but today its definition is concentrated on exploring the meaning of knowledge and our relationship with the universe.

Psychoanalysis A discipline that studies the unconscious mind. Pioneered by Sigmund Freud (1856-1939), who investigated unconscious repressed desires and the mental illnesses they can cause.

Protagonist Originally, the leading actor in an ancient Greek tragedy. It is a term more generally applied today to the principle character in a novel, short story or play.

Rananim The name given by Lawrence to the Utopian society he wished to create with a few select friends.

Realism An approach to literature and art in which effort is concentrated on showing life and things in general as they are seen to be by the artist. It is often associated with an unsentimental outlook.

Ritual Carrying out formal customs, especially associated with religions.

Romantic movement An artistic movement begun in the late eighteenth century which exulted the imagination and spirit of man, praising what was wild and noble in nature and despising the artificial and merely intellectual.

Symbolism An artistic technique in which objects, images or words are used to represent more than one meaning. An object becomes a symbol when it is used to suggest deeper meaning or hidden depths.

Tuberculosis A disease, also called consumption; which causes a wasting away of the affected part of the body (usually the lungs).

Utopia An ideal way of life or a term used to describe a community in which this ideal could be achieved. The word actually means 'nowhere', and was coined by Thomas More for the title of his book written on the philosophical nature of such societies in 1516.

Working class Traditionally, those in a capitalist society who have to sell their labour to earn their living.

List of Dates

1885	D H Lawrence born, 11 September, in Victoria Street, Eastwood, Nottinghamshire.
1892	Attends Beauvale Board School.
1898	Attends Nottingham High School.
1901	For three months works as a clerk at a surgical appliance factory. Becomes seriously ill with pneumonia.
	Death of his brother, Ernest.
	Meets Jessie Chambers at Haggs Farm.
1902	Becomes a pupil-teacher at the British School, Eastwood.
1904	Takes a course for pupil-teachers at Ilkeston.
	Forms an intellectual circle called the Pagans. Members include fellow teachers, Jessie Chambers and Louie Burrows.
1905	First poems.
1906	At Nottingham University College for two-year teacher-training course.
	Begins *The White Peacock*.
1907	'A Prelude' published in the *Nottinghamshire Guardian*.
1908	Teacher in Croydon, Surrey.
	Meets Helen Corke.
1909	Writes 'Odour of Chrysanthemums'.
	Poems published in *The English Review*, edited by Ford Madox Ford.
1910	Death of his mother.
	Becomes engaged to Louie Burrows.
	Completes *The White Peacock*.
	Begins 'The Trespasser' and 'Paul Morel' (later to be called *Sons and Lovers*).
1911	'The White Peacock' is published.
	Writes 'The Daughters of the Vicar'.
	Meets Edward Garnett, editor of the *Century*.
	Another serious attack of pnuemonia.
	Writes the play *The Collier's Friday Night*.
1912	Leaves teaching. Meets Frieda Weekly and elopes with her to Germany and Italy.
	'The Trespasser' published.
	Sons and Lovers is finished.
1913	Returns to England with Frieda.

Breaks relations with Jessie Chambers.
Meets John Middleton Murray and Katherine Mansfield.
Publishes *Love Poems and Others,* and *Sons and Lovers.*
Goes back to Europe. Begins work on 'The Sisters' (Later to became *The Rainbow* and *Women in Love*) and 'The Lost Girl'.

1914   Outbreak of the First World War.
Marries Frieda, 13 July in England. Meets Lady Ottoline Morrell.
'The Widowing of Mrs Holroyd' and 'The Prussian Officer' published.
Moves to Chesham, Buckinghamshire.

1915   *The Rainbow* published. Suppressed almost immediately. Edits *The Signature*, with Murray and Mansfield. Meets Aldous Huxley. Plans a series of lectures on the War with Bertrand Russell.
Lives at Pulborough, Sussex and in London.
Writes *A Study of Thomas Hardy.*

1916   Living at Zennor in Cornwall.
Finishes *Women in Love.*
Twilight in Italy published.
Twice medically examined for military service. Declared unfit.

1917   Frieda and Lawrence expelled from Cornwall as suspected spies.
Moves to Chapel Farm cottage in Berkshire, and London.
Look! We Have Come Through published.
Aaron's Rod begun.

1918   Moves to Mountain Cottage, Derbyshire.
3rd medical examination.
New Poems and *Studies in Classic American Literature* published.
Writes 'The Fox'.

1919   Departs for the Continent.
Living in Italy.
Publishes *Bay: A Book of Poems.*

1920   *Women in Love* published in New York.
'The Lost Girl' published in London. (Awarded the James Tait Black Memorial prize.)
Living in Taormina, Sicily.

1921   Travels in Sardinia, Germany and Capri.
Writes 'The Captain's Doll' and 'The

Ladybird'.
Publishes *Movements in European History*, *Psychoanalysis and the Unconscious*, *Sea and Sardinia*.

1922 Moves on to Ceylon, Australia, California and New Mexico.
Settles at ranch near Taos, New Mexico. Begins *Kangaroo*.
Aaron's Road, *Fantasia of the Unconscious*, *England, My England* all published.

1923 Visits Mexico. His father dies. *The Plumed Serpent* begun.
'The Ladybird', *Studies in Classic American Literature*, *Kangaroo*, *Birds, Beasts and Flowers* all published.

1924 Returns to New Mexico.
Seriously ill with tuberculosis.
Revisits Mexico.
'The Boy in the Bush' published.

1925 Brief visit to London. Settles in Florence.
'The Woman who Rode Away', and 'The Princess' begun.
'St. Mawr' and *Reflections on the Death of a Porcupine* published.

1926 *Lady Chatterley's Lover* begun.
The Plumed Serpent published.

1927 Visits Etruria. *Mornings in Mexico* published.

1928 Visits Switzerland and France. 'The Man Who Died' written.
'The Woman Who Rode Away', *Lady Chatterley's Lover*, *Collected Poems*, published.

1929 In France, Majorca, Germany and back to France.
Paintings seized by police at exhibition at Warren Galleries, London.
Manuscript of *Pansies* seized by customs.
Writes *A Propos of Lady Chatterley's Lover*, *Apocalypse* and 'The Ship of Death'.
Pansies published.

1930 Dies at Vence, southern France, 2 March.

1931 *Apocalypse* published.

1932 *Etruscan Places*, *The Letters* (ed. Aldous Huxley), *Last Poems* published.

1933 *The Ship of Death* published.

1935 *Phoenix* published.
His ashes are moved to a specially built chapel at Kiowa Ranch, New Mexico.

Further Reading

Lawrence's novels and short stories are all available in Penguin paperbacks.

Biography & Criticism
CLARKE, C. *A Casebook* (*The Rainbow* and *Women in Love*) (Macmillan, 1969)
HOUGH, G. *The Dark Sun: A Study of D.H. Lawrence* (Duckworth, 1956)
LAWRENCE, F. *Not I, But the Wind* (Granada, 1983)
LEAVIS, F.R. *D.H. Lawrence: Novelist* (Chatto & Windus, 1955)
MOORE, H.T. (ed.) *The Collected Letters of D.H. Lawrence* (Heinemann, 1962)
SAGAR, K. *D.H. Lawrence: Life into Art* (Penguin, 1985)
SAGAR, K. *The Life of D.H. Lawrence* (Methuen, 1980)
SALGADO, G. (ed.) *A Casebook (Sons and Lovers)* (Macmillan, 1969)
SALGADO, G. *A Preface to Lawrence* (Longman, 1986)

Picture acknowledgements

The author and publishers would like to thank the following for allowing their illustrations to be reproduced in this book: Mary Evans Picture Library 9, 10, 34, 36, 45, 46, 59, 61, 63, 64, 67, 75; the National Film Archive 49, 55, 56, 73, 74, 77, 79; the University of Nottingham Library 6, 8, 12, 13, 14, 15, 16, 17, 19, 20, 21, 22, 23, 24, 25, 26, 27, 29, 31, 32, 33, 37, 39, 41, 42, 44, 50, 53, 66, 68, 71, 80, 82, 83, 84, 85, 87, 88, 90, 95, 96, 99. All other pictures are from the Wayland Picture Library. The original painting on page 95 is owned by Broxtowe Borough Council, and is on view at the D. H. Lawrence Birthplace Museum, Eastwood, Nottinghamshire.

Index